END BULLYING BEFORE IT ENDS A LIFE

STOP BULLYING NOW!

ONE HUNDRED BLOGS AND COLORFUL PICTURES ON ERADICATING WORKPLACE BULLYING

CLARA WAJNGURT

BOOK DESIGNER, SARA J. CUBAS

NEWMAN SPRINGS PUBLISHING
320 Broad Street
Red Bank, NJ 07701

First originally published by Newman Springs Publishing 2022

ISBN 978-1-63692-623-0 (Paperback)
ISBN 978-1-63692-624-7 (Digital)

Printed in the United States of America

ACKNOWLEDGMENTS

First, I am dedicating this book to my children, Avrohom and Esther, who are very interested in improving the world by making the world a better place to live in and serving as a mentor and leader for others. I am thanking my husband, David, who has given me his unconditional support to advance research in workplace bullying, and who related stories about bullying in his and his peers' experiences. I am especially thankful to Josie and Liz, who have worked with me endlessly on adding pictures, formatting, and structuring my blogs on social media, and with this I am especially appreciative and acknowledge Shutterstock's contribution to the pictures presented in this book, which makes this book so unique.

Lastly, I want to thank my friend Maria, who has helped me with every contribution I have done and has contributed greatly to all my successes.

PREFACE

I write about workplace bullying because bullying has reached epidemic proportions in our workplaces. We need to stop the bullies who control the workplace, to the point of destroying their colleagues' self-esteem and causing many to leave. It is time to do some self-analysis in our workplaces and to look at any bullying behavior that has occurred there and to stop this cycle. I have seen enough bullying in and out of the workplace and it must be stopped!

I am inspired to do this research on workplace bullying so that we can look forward to going to work and to acting civilly with one another.

INTRODUCTION

The author writes a monthly blog on social media. This book is the culmination of blogs written over a two-year period. The idea is to create awareness about bullying and to educate those who get bullied about what to do when this happens.

CONTENTS

CHAPTER 1

Bullying
The Problem

#1 BULLYING IN THE WORKPLACE

Bullying in the workplace is costly to everyone concerned. When the bullied worker is unhappy, it is possible for the worker to develop mental and physical symptoms as a response to the bullying. Workplace bullying has a detrimental effect on all employees who work. The anxiety, disengagement, dissatisfaction, and distraction felt by the employee who is bullied resonates with everyone who works. Essentially, employees in this case dread the return each day to a job that is characteristic of high stress, misdirected bosses, and narrow budgets. Now let's add to this scenario the boss who bullies and who victimizes the staff by making unexpected changes to projects with given deadlines, especially during challenging times on the job, and who also insults the staff when orders are not followed.

Clearly the climate in this job scenario must be changed—and when incivility, bullying, discrimination, and harassment exist on the job, the workplace environment becomes unhealthy. This behavior from bully to the one who is bullied, occurring on the job, eventually becomes costly to any workplace.

#2 WHY SHOULD WE TALK ABOUT WORKPLACE BULLYING?

Workplace bullying behavior is defined as "offensive, intimidating, malicious or insulting behavior which deliberately intends to dominate, cause distress and fear over a period of time, to the one who is being bullied" (Agarwal 2018). The person who is bullied is scared and worried to talk about it to someone because talking about it can cause trouble, or maybe the one who was bullied is not sure that the behaviors are really bullying behaviors.

The bullying can have a negative impact on one's work performance and detrimental effects on one's physical and mental health. One becomes more worried, more anxious, and miserable about going to work. Being bullied at work erodes one's self-esteem, wearing down the person who is bullied, so much that they are less trusting of their own instincts and judgments about their performance.

So this is why we need to talk about bullying in the workplace. By talking confidentially about our experiences in the workplace and feelings about workplace bullying, we will relieve some tension and anxiety and find help to deal more positively with our jobs. If an ombudsperson or human resources person can fulfill this need, that would be great. Otherwise, we alone need to start this process of healing others who have been affected by workplace bullying through talking, instructing, and reaching out to those in need.

#3 WHY DOES WORKPLACE BULLYING REALLY OCCUR?

I read an article recently about why bullying occurs. For children and adolescents, we find bullying behavior is "rooted in the discrimination of someone seen as culturally or physically different or socially less" (Rodriguez-Hidalgo et al. 2019). Adults who bully adults do not have these reasons for bullying necessarily but tend to target those perceived as threats. Bullying is essentially seen as a top-down hierarchical approach that encourages a culture of incivility often manifested through overt and covert forms of aggression dealing with interpersonal mistreatment and harassment. This occurs especially in academic settings where people challenge power bases and incur marginalization and targeting. Hierarchical settings reinforce a culture of humiliation and antagonization, existing often with abusive and repressive actions.

Those in hierarchical settings like hospital settings having doctors versus nurses or higher education settings having deans versus professors must learn to engage in behaviors that do not reflect bullying. This is why a bullying prevention statement ought to exist in especially such workplace settings.

Do you think this will help?

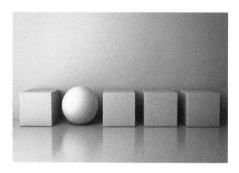

#4 CHANGES IN OUR WORKPLACE ENVIRONMENTS

Our work environments are changing rapidly, and we should be attuned to such changes. The Forbes Coaches Council has focused on some outdated managerial practices (October 2019):

1. Our workplaces are becoming more virtual, which means employees can work from almost anywhere. Some leaders have a mindset that if they don't see you in the office, then you are not working. Managerial leaders must focus on results, not on physical presence.
2. Forget the annual performance review! Business moves more quickly, so feedback should move along similarly. Give your employees feedback as often as possible. Instead of being a manager, become a coach and give ongoing feedback. In this way, your team can make immediate improvements to their work.
3. Competency use to be a way to assess knowledge. But when someone is competent in one area, they may miss the full picture and are then less open to innovative changes. In today's marketplace, agility—the ability to move quickly and easily and the capacity to understand fully—has become more pronounced.
4. Today we prefer more immediate communications. We use social media, texting, and engaging our colleagues via mobile tools. The idea is to stay in touch, engaged, and to provide real-time feedback.

5. Stop focusing on weaknesses. This makes it harder to achieve effective results. Concentrate on strengths, and work with these characteristics on your team. Develop a positive attitude to work.

6. Command and control leadership was effective when certain individuals were accountable for producing certain results. Now we are looking for shared leadership and collaboration. Teams now have multiple leaders with a shared purpose. A leader will demonstrate to the team that it's okay to make mistakes, especially when we are sincere and accountable to one another.

7. The idea is to appreciate different viewpoints and encourage animated discussion, not to seek full consensus from your team.

These changes to our workplace environment should decrease workplace bullying.

#5 TRENDS IN THE WORKPLACE FOR THE TWENTY-FIRST CENTURY SHOULD DECREASE WORKPLACE BULLYING IF IMPLEMENTED

We need to think of ways to stop workplace bullying. As a manager or supervisor, we need to think of ways that will minimize, if not eradicate, such behaviors. As our workplaces are becoming more diverse and accepting of different situations—part-timers, full-timers, stay-at-home workers, workers in the office, etc.—our workplace trends are changing in the twenty-first century.

Are we creating a more sensitive workplace (Vozza 2019)?

1. There are now more opportunities for flexible work as a result of emerging technologies so that the original 9:00 a.m.–5:00 p.m. design is changing, and more flexible arrangements are being accounted. Work opportunities are becoming more remote, and the pool of candidates is becoming more expansive, where colleagues are coming from different geographical locations. This can increase morale and decrease commuting times to get to work.

2. More emphasis on diversity and inclusion has led to different perspectives and more creativity. Many organizations have built-in programs that recognize potential bias, and there are more supports and training to be inclusive in the workforce.

3. There are more objective formulas for salary, where pay is becoming more transparent. In this way, companies can diminish biases and overt inequality in salaries between men and women. A company must be held accountable to achieving such standards.

4. Renewed focus on skills where on-the-job training and skills development are becoming more commonplace in the work environment. Mentoring of coworkers is on the rise.

5. Employees want to find work that is meaningful and that has a purpose. In this way, there are higher levels of job satisfaction for everyone on the job.

#6 EMPATHIC LEADERS TACKLE THOSE WHO ARE BULLIED

Empathy is the ability to experience and relate to the thoughts, emotions, and experiences of others (Pressley 2012). When your friend empathizes with you, your friend basically feels and thinks what you are feeling. In the workplace, when your colleague exhibits empathy towards others on the job, your colleague shows that he/she cares for others.

An empathic leader in the workplace is one who makes everyone feel they are part of the team. As a result of this feeling, the team will then exhibit positive morale and loyalty towards one another. When leaders are empathic, they like people, value people as individuals, and enjoy working with and helping others.

If an individual on your team has been bullied, the empathic leader will listen, will be open, and will understand what the one who is bullied feels. In this way, the empathic leader helps struggling colleagues on the team to improve productivity on the job.

We need to encourage more empathic leaders in our workplaces.

#7 HOW DOES ONE CREATE EMPATHIC COLLEAGUES IN THE WORKPLACE?

Empathy is an ability for one colleague to understand and share the feelings of another colleague. Very often we work with colleagues who can be uncivil and disrespectful. It is important to listen carefully to one another and to show support. Also at the root of empathy is showing compassion for one another. When a coworker feels bullied, stay away from being a bystander and work with your colleague who feels bullied. Try to encourage loyalty and productivity in your workplace.

How does one create empathy in the workplace (Barnhart 2020)?

1. When your colleagues come to you with questions and comments, how well are you listening? It is not enough to be a good listener, but make yourself as available as possible to solve issues and concerns. Be proactive in solving problems.
2. Ask the right questions to get at the root of understanding what the issues are. It's not enough to say, "I hear you. What can I do to help?" Ask for details so you can help solve the problem with your coworker. Get to the root of the problem and work on solutions proactively.
3. Try to put yourself in your colleague's shoes. If your colleague feels frustrated and is snapping back, tell them you also feel this way periodically. Diffuse the situation by offering to help work on this together.

4. Give people the benefit of the doubt. If a colleague doesn't follow workplace policy, assume this person doesn't know.
5. Prioritize and stay organized.
6. Support your coworkers and stay away from critique and condescending comments. In this way, we will value our areas of employment and look forward to coming to work each day.

#8 HOW COMMON IS WORKPLACE BULLYING?

Recently I read that Alana Van Gundy, professor of justice and community studies at Miami University in Ohio, distributed a survey and asked faculty members how often they had witnessed or had been the target of aggressive behaviors (Gluckman 2017). Some of these behaviors could include eye-rolling, shouting, humiliation, or rumor spreading.

Out of 830 people, she received the following:

- 64 percent of the respondents said they had been the target of faculty incivility, while 77 percent of the respondents said they had witnessed someone else being targeted.
- 71 percent of those targeted reported the incivility or aggression to a colleague, but 50 percent of the time the incivility or aggression continued in spite of their report.

- Nearly 50 percent of those targeted were tenured.

- 64% of those who bullied had been accused of incivility or bullying in the past, and nearly 44% of those accused of bullying in the past had been accused of such action five or more times.

It is amazing that almost half of those accused of bullying have done the same action five or more times. Our educational system needs to look at each of the individuals doing the bullying and to educate them on the negatives of these actions. We need to study mechanisms that can implement the end of bullying.

#9 ORGANIZATIONAL CLIMATE, ORGANIZATIONAL CULTURE, AND WORKPLACE BULLYING

Organizational climate and organizational culture seem very connected when dealing with acts of bullying.

Organizational climate is a measure of the quality of an atmosphere as perceived by members in the organization that other employees perceive and how members evaluate experiences within that particular work environment (Forte 2011). The organizational climate reflects norms, attitudes, behaviors, and feelings of an organization. For example, a boss who is open to change and innovative ideas or a boss who is perceived as threatening to change or controlling is part of the organizational climate.

Leadership style affects employee behavior and thinking and emotional responses to the workplace which affect the organizational climate.

Organizational culture is a measure of the quality of social interactions that develop when people in the group interact (James and McIntyre 1996). The organizational culture deals with the existing distance between bosses and their colleagues. What impact does this have on organizational issues? How are memos, reports, rules, and regulations solved, individually or in a shared manner? Are there gender stereotypical roles among the bosses? How does the organization achieve its goals? How much autonomy do employees have? Is the structure hierarchical or characteristic of rigid lines of communication?

Organizational climate is a perception of interactions, while organizational culture is a construct that actually guides behavior. In the middle of this discussion is how workplace bullying impacts organizational climate and organizational culture in the workplace.

#10 WORKPLACE CULTURE AND ORGANIZATIONAL CULTURE

Workplace culture or organizational culture sets the tone for your organization. It includes how your colleagues relate to one another, how businesses are run, whether the climate is toxic or not, and how comfortable people feel. Some further points about workplace culture:

- When building the culture at your company, lead by example, define your values, and have a purpose or goal about how you want to accomplish what you need.
- The culture of your organization should be aligned with your basic beliefs and goals of the organization.
- Build trust and encourage team building by maintaining feedback with your colleagues. Establish a working collaborative environment.
- Keep a balance between positive and negative emotions. Engage in conflict resolution, and acknowledge mistakes and move forward.
- Bring everyone to the table so that diversity and inclusion are honored. Encourage civility in your organization. A productive workplace culture will reduce workplace bullying.

#11 EXPLORING THE NATURE OF BULLYING: DIFFERENT TYPES OF BULLIES

What I'd like to do in this blog is to explore the nature of bullying and discuss according to Olweus the three different types of bullies:

Aggressive bullies is the most common type of bully. Such people tend to be physically strong, impulsive, hot-tempered, belligerent, and fearless. Their personality is characterized by aggression, motivated by a quest for power and a desire to dominate others. Often they see negative characteristics in people around them, especially when such traits don't even exist.

Passive bullies tend to be more insecure than the aggressive bully. The passive bully tends to have low self-esteem. Some may have difficulty focusing their attention on projects and are prone to violent outbursts or temper tantrums. Often passive bullies show loyalty to aggressive bullies.

Bully targets are bullies who have been targets of bullying themselves. The bully target tends to have a weaker personality than the other two types of bullies but are found to be stronger than the aggressive or passive bully. The bully target is easily aroused and provokes others, especially those who are weaker than the bully target.

Wolke (1999) mentioned that there are pure bullies who do not fall into any of these categories—bully, target or bully target—and the claim is they just use bullying to dominate others.

#12 WORKPLACE BULLIES THRIVE BECAUSE OF BYSTANDERS

We have heard time and time again that workplace bullies thrive because of the bystanders, who watch the bullying take place.

The bystander effect occurs in a situation that shows when a person (or target) needs help and observes simply, standing by and doesn't assist the target. Very often when there are many observers to workplace bullying on the job, people will say either "I am too afraid to get involved" or "someone else will help, it's not my responsibility."

The first step to overcome the bystander effect is to recognize that a problem exists, the target needs help, and a bully is exacerbating the situation. Once we recognize that a problem exists, then help is needed to alleviate the situation.

Secondly, the bystander must be confident that they can make a difference in the situation, do something to help out.

Very often when the bystanders complain to their supervisors about a workplace bullying incident, it can backfire because the supervisor will not call this bullying and will not respect the actual complaint.

If your organization was better informed, perhaps had a workplace bullying prevention policy, bystanders would not be afraid to speak up for fear they might lose their jobs.

In this case, they would be more apt to support the one who is bullied. What do you think?

#13 BYSTANDER RESPONSES

Recently (August 2018) I read an article in the *Chronicle of Higher Education* (Vaillancourt) about our role as a bystander in the higher education setting. Certainly when we are hired, we know that we have an obligation to help our students succeed and to perform department and college functions, which advance our discipline and our college. But what do we do when we have colleagues who exhibit intimidating behavior or behavior that bullies others? If we remain silent, that sounds like we are complicit in this unethical and disrespectful behavior, and perhaps the bully will continue this behavior if we do nothing. If you speak up, you might damage relationships in your department, or such action on your part may even affect your career goals if the bully is an administrator high on the organizational chart or a full professor. In these cases, the bully might retaliate.

Maybe we need some lessons in being an upstander by using certain strategies that intervene and shift the dynamics of the situation. One can say, "Let's continue with this after the meeting," if someone makes a derogatory remark during a meeting, or one can ask the target to expand on what was being suggested. If someone is being bullied in front of us, are we prepared to say something to the point of diffusing the situation so that your position is not compromised?

Is this possible? What do you think?

Clara Wajngurt

#14 ARE YOU A GOOD LISTENER?

Are you a good listener? Being a great listener (Perlmutter 2019) is essential for most jobs. Being able to hear and understand what people are saying through their words, tone, manner, and body language is vital for succeeding in any management and leadership position. How do we learn the basics of listening to others? Don't just listen. Show you are listening. Many people have habits like wandering eyes, fidgeting, tapping fingers, etc., cutting off a speaker in midsentence. It is important for the person whom you are talking to, to perceive you are listening. If you jump into a cutoff sentence, you appear as impatient, inattentive, and a poor listener. Often people want acknowledgment that someone cared enough to listen to what they said. Identify key words and phrases especially when people come to your office with long lists of things to say. In this case, stop the speaker at an appropriate point and say, "Let's review what you just said. I see your point about X." Get the salient points of the conversation.

Let's think of examples where listening is important.

Try to understand what behaviors are implicit. Detect codes and symbols. For example, a provost may be hesitant to say to his chair for political reasons, "Your unit is low on the priority list for funding." Instead the provost will say, "We need to keep an eye on your departmental budget, and we look forward to working with you." It is very important to read between the lines. After you have listened and valued the conversation, follow up to see how the person is doing, how they feel after the conversation. With honed listening skills, we should better handle workplace bullying incidents as they arise.

#15 HOW TO HAVE A DIFFICULT CONVERSATION

I recently read an excellent article, "Four Things to Do before a Tough Conversation" (Grenny 2019). It is about how we as managers, supervisors, staff, and others have to grapple with difficult judgments and decisions throughout the course of our work lives.

A quick example, Randy has been working at a company for nine years. His work output has been marginal, but he is likable and sociable. His team is in a state of disarray because they have not gotten the proper leadership from Randy. The manager is having a conversation with Randy at 2:00 p.m., where she plans to fire him. How do you as a manager approach this?

What to do? Does the manager concentrate on her concerns and whether she is clear to Randy? The success you have with such conversations is dependent more on what you do before you have this important conversation.

- *Get your motives straight.* By avoiding conflict with Randy over the years and hearing incessant complaints from Randy's coworkers, the manager compromised her ability to save Randy's job, frustrated the team, and lost customers. Ask yourself the following: What do I really want? What do I want for me? What do I want for my other colleagues? What do I want for my customers?
- *Get your emotions straight.* Should the manager come to the conversation angry, hurt, or defensive? Should the manager behave as a victim, with an attitude "I could have helped Randy more"? Or should

I make Randy into a villain, "Well, Randy did not fix his situation. He is just lazy and unmotivated."

Stay away from the victim and villain stories. Become an actor and treat Randy with respect. Ask yourself the following: What am I pretending not to know about my role in this? How does a rational person behave in Randy's situation? What is expected here?

- *Gather the facts.* The conversation is starting with opposing viewpoints. I am getting Randy fired, and Randy wants to stay. Share the facts that led up to this conclusion. Describe the data you have. Build your case patiently and honestly.
- *Be curious.* Bring to this conversation confidence. Listen to what Randy has to say. Be open to information that might persuade your decision. By having this attitude, we can all approach our difficult conversations in a more mature manner.

#16 HOW TO STOP WORKPLACE GOSSIP IN YOUR OFFICE

What can we do to stop all that gossip and negative verbiage (bullying) towards others in your office?

First start with yourself and extend these tips to all people in your organization from top leaders to staff:

1. Define bullying.
2. Write a policy about workplace bullying prevention.
3. Make sure these policies are implemented by others.
4. Be aware of your own behavior so that you do not bully others or others do not bully you.
5. When you see bullying occurring, let others know that someone is being bullied. Become an upstander!
6. Stop the bullying when it happens. Speak up.
7. Prevent the bullying from occurring again. Make sure workplace bullying policies are implemented.

What do you think?

#17 IS FEAR THE BIGGEST FACTOR IN REPORTING WORKPLACE BULLYING?

Recently I heard a report on the BBC news back in January 2020 that the Chartered Institute of Personnel Development in London, England, claimed that a quarter of employees think their company turns a blind eye to workplace bullying and harassment. Why are the statistics (25 percent) so high? Fact: people who are bullied do not even report it to their workplaces or simply do nothing about it. It is assumed that fear is the biggest factor in reporting workplace bullying, because the bully has singled out a target and the target feels violated. In addition, the target can suffer from stress, anxiety, insomnia, among many conditions, which paralyze the target emotionally as a result of this bullying. It takes courage for people to speak up about inappropriate behavior at work, and the problem is that organizations do not have the processes to deal with such issues effectively. Very often people do not know to whom or how to report such incidents. When a person on the job is being undermined or humiliated, criticized constantly, or described through unwanted personal remarks, it is important to speak up about such behaviors. Create a procedure for resolving complaints on the job. Research shows that managers who receive training on inappropriate workplace behaviors are more effective in encouraging healthy workplace relationships.

Clara Wajngurt

#18 GASLIGHTING

I read about gaslighting at work from David Yamada's blog, and it was defined to be a "form of deliberate manipulation intended to disorient, confuse and frighten those on the receiving end." One can see then how the bully can confuse and frighten its target with antics that distort and upset the one who is bullied.

As Yamada points out in the book of Stern's *The Gaslight Effect: How to Spot and Survive the Hidden Manipulation Others Use to Control Your Life*, gaslighting is a type of emotional manipulation in which a gaslighter (like a bully) tries to convince its target that the target is misremembering, misunderstanding, or misinterpreting one's (the target's) behavior, creating doubt in one's mind that leaves the target vulnerable and confused.

Bullying incidents cause the one who is bullied to not only feel confused about themselves and their workplace environment but cause the targeted person to feel that they want to escape and not appear at their jobs. It appears that gaslighting is a form of bullying behavior, which should be avoided at all costs.

#19 GASLIGHTING VERSUS EMPATHY

Bullying is about power and control. When bullies find a target for their terrorized behavior, the bully will do all it can to maintain their dominance and authority. This is all done at the target's expense. In the process of bullying the target, the bully may manipulate the target through psychological means, whereby the target will doubt his/her sanity. This is called gaslighting. For example, this can occur when the bully lies about some project and tries to convince the target that the target is mentally unstable and does not know the full picture, or the bully will simply say to the target, "I'm not bullying you. You're overly sensitive." This causes confusion, anxiety, and shame for the target.

Assert yourself and confront the bully. Tell others about the bully's behavior so they won't become targets of the bully.

Let's encourage our workplaces to work in more empathic environments so that the people who work around us have the ability to sense other colleague's emotions. In this way, we can better understand what our colleagues are thinking and feeling.

This will definitely lead to more productive and healthy work environments.

#20 WORKPLACE HAZARDS: WHO IS RESPONSIBLE?

I went to an OSHA (Occupational Safety and Health Act) workshop the other day. We learned about Workplace Safety and Health Hazards. They included the following:

1. *General safety hazards.* Falling, working with sharp objects, slipping, fire hazards, etc.
2. *Biological hazards.* Mold fungus, infectious diseases, like tuberculosis, coronavirus, insects, etc.
3. *Ergonomic hazards.* Lifting (heavy boxes), back strain, standing all day, maintaining awkward postures, etc.
4. *Psychological/Stress hazards.* Heavy workloads, long work hours, violent colleagues, workplace violence, etc.
5. *Chemical hazards.* Existence of lead, asbestos, formaldehyde, fumes, etc.
6. *Physical hazards.* Noise, poor lighting, lack of ventilation, poor temperatures, etc.

Workplace bullying falls under psychological hazards. It is important for our workplaces to encourage its colleagues to prevent accidents, and to protect the health and safety of our colleagues.

#21 ORGANIZATIONAL AND SAFETY COMMITMENT

Academic and corporate environments are continually searching for techniques to decrease risk exposure for their employees. The company's or university's approach to which safety standards are implemented and enforced can impact employee attitudes towards their organization. Safety commitment deals with management's efforts to demonstrate safety as a priority in the workplace. This includes an end to workplace violence behaviors. Workplace commitment on the part of an employee can affect one's attitude or expression to workplace violence. Organizational commitment deals with affection for your job, a fear of losing your job, or a sense of obligation to staying on your job. If one is a target of workplace violence, one's organizational commitment to their job is not strong because management does not show a serious commitment to safety on the job. If management allows bullies to thrive on a job, then the environment does not respect safety for its employees.

We need to encourage management to focus on safety procedures and policies that are implemented for their employees.

#22 WHAT IS EXPECTED IN AN INVESTIGATION OF WORKPLACE BULLYING?

How does one perform an investigation for a workplace bullying incident?

1. Make sure your employees know in your department that there will be an investigation.
2. Who will conduct this investigation?
3. How will the complaint be investigated? What materials are needed, who is coming, etc., if this is done in person or what data is needed?
4. What are the rights of the involved parties to representation?
5. Establish a timeline for the investigation?
6. What is the mechanism for appealing a decision?
7. All parties should focus on resolving the situation, not on blaming parties.
8. Be fair and equitable by allowing the bully, target, and bystanders to respond.
9. Ensure confidentiality of all parties.
10. Make sure that a quick resolution is facilitated.

If these steps resolve workplace bullying incidents, we believe that the process will be an effective one.

#23 WHEN DOES WORKPLACE BULLYING BECOME WORKPLACE VIOLENCE?

I heard about a student nurse who tried to get a blood pressure reading on a postoperative patient in recovery, and the on-call surgeon verbally scolded the student nurse in front of staff because she was not taking the blood pressure quickly. This example demonstrates uncivil behavior of a doctor towards a nurse. If done repetitively, it turns into workplace bullying. If it appears that the doctor is about to assault the nurse, this is workplace violence.

Another time the same nurse was choked by a patient's father when the nurse asked the father to leave the hospital room at midnight, well after visiting hours were over. The attack caused no physical harm to the nurse but left a mental mark. This behavior demonstrates workplace violence.

Workplace violence is defined by OSHA guidelines (Occupational Safety and Health Administration) as "violence or the threat of violence, physical assault or threats of assault directed toward persons at work or on duty. It can range from verbal abuse (which appears violent) to homicide."

We need to recognize workplace violence when it occurs on the job. It is recommended that the employer establish a workplace violence prevention program for their employees.

Workplace safety should be of paramount importance to everyone on the job. OSHA requires employers to provide a safe and healthy workplace for all workers on the job.

#24 WHAT IS WORKPLACE VIOLENCE?

Lately I've been writing about workplace violence, and the fact is, it includes workplace bullying. So I'd like to present the different definitions of workplace violence in the literature. The one I have seen the most emphasized is the one by NIOSH (National Institute for Occupational Safety and Health), which includes violent acts (including physical assaults and threats of assaults) directed towards persons at work or on duty.

I have also seen the following as definitions of workplace violence:

1. Attacks and threats against a victim by someone in the workplace (Cooper and Swanson 2002)
2. Any activity that causes hostility and has physical and psychological adverse effects on the employees in an organization (Cooper and Swanson 2002)
3. All kinds of physical attacks, threatening behavior, or abusive words in the workplace (Niosh 2002)

Just from these definitions we can see how workplace bullying is part of workplace violence, and these behaviors must be stopped.

#25 CYBERBULLYING

Cyberbullying is a form of bullying that uses technology. It can be done through the computer, smartphone devices, or any form of electronic communication. It includes rumors, threats, inappropriate communication, or the improper use of personal information about the target that degrades and debases the target. Sometimes the cyberbully does this to elicit a reaction from its target or just for the unfortunate personal enjoyment on the part of the cyberbully. Most often the target cannot defend oneself as the focus of sending and posting texts or images of the target, which are intended to hurt the target. These texts or images can be transferred quickly by electronic communication throughout all computers in the world. It harasses someone through repeated threats, sexual innuendos, ridicule, or false accusations that serve to humiliate the targeted person through electronic communication.

Cyberbullying occurs on social media sites, like Twitter, Instagram, Facebook, etc., and can involve passive-aggressive postings on work sites and negative comments from clients in the corporate world or faculty and staff in the academic world. Particularly the internet allows bullies to hide behind their computer screens and to say things online that they may not say directly in person.

We need to create policies on the job against bullying and cyberbullying.

#26 END RESULTS OF BEING BULLIED

The end result of being bullied in the workplace:

- The bullied person feels that they were not heard nor respected.
- There was a lack of team support.
- Civility, collegiality, and friendship were diminished on the team.
- The bullied person may ignore, withdraw, or give in to the bully.
- Work productivity decreases.
- Stress levels increase.

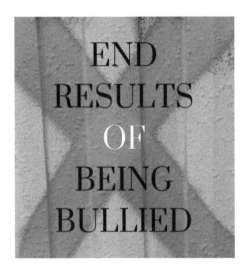

#27 WHAT TO KNOW BEFORE ACCEPTING A JOB OFFER

You get an interview and you are excited you are accepted for the job. But there are several things you must check before you accept a job offer:

1. *Company culture.* How do you describe it? What is the vision of your organization? How do coworkers treat one another / how do they interact?
2. *The people.* Do they seem friendly to you? Can you pick up if they are ethical? Have you read company reviews?
3. *Your responsibilities.* Is the head of the hiring team telling you explicitly what your role will be? How does the job description match your role? Will you have a personal life with this job? Will you be bored at this job?
4. *Expectations.* Are there reachable targets and goals on your job, or do you get unrealistic workloads?
5. *Opportunities.* What happened to the last person who held this position? Is the culture competitive? Where do you expect me to be in five years?
6. *Training.* Will you be trained if you cannot do a procedure? What kind of support do you have?
7. *Salary and benefits.* Try to negotiate, especially if you have prior experience.
8. *Job commute.* If it takes you a long time to get to the job: "I may be tired, nonfunctioning." Try to determine these points by asking others on the job or with those who previously left, or at your interview, in order to increase your job satisfaction and decrease any malaise.

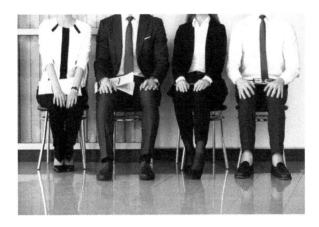

Clearly the climate in this job scenario must be changed when incivility, bullying, discrimination and harassment, exist on the job, or if the workplace environment becomes unhealthy. This behavior from bully to the one who is bullied, occurring on the job, eventually becomes costly to any workplace.

CHAPTER 2

Bullying
Physical And Mental Effects

#28 HARMFUL EFFECTS OF WORKPLACE BULLYING

We know that today there are millions of people who are targeted by workplace bullying on their jobs. As a result, targets of bullying can have deteriorating health that is caused by the destructive behavior of a boss, coworker or a group of coworkers.

So what could happen if one is bullied in the workplace?

1. *Mental health suffers.* People who suffer from bullying day in and day out deal with stress that takes a toll on one's body. Sometimes a target can suffer from post-traumatic stress disorder, panic attacks, anxiety, depression, or paranoia. These disorders can lead to other deleterious health problems, like drug and alcohol abuse.

2. *Physical health suffers.* People who suffer from bullying day in and day out can have physical ailments, stressing parts of their body which impact on the person's immune system—more colds, migraine headaches, irritable bowel syndrome, high blood pressure, and chest pain.

3. *Bystanders suffer.* People who observe the bully-
    ing can suffer these physical and mental effects as
    well. It is possible that people who witness bully-
    ing become distressed by the adverse hostility even
    if they don't recognize or experience the bullying
    directly.
4. *Work performance suffer.* People who are targeted
    or who serve as bystanders to workplace bullying
    are negatively impacted by the bullying. Bullying a
    target causes the target to feel low self-esteem and
    to experience poor decision-making with regard to
    job tasks.

There is a lack of motivation and a desire to avoid the
job. Anyone who observes bullying incidents can suffer as
well.

Don't you think we need to stop this process?

#29 WORKPLACE BULLYING AND TRAUMA

Trauma is a highly stressful experience that can result in permanent or temporary physical and emotional effects. When a person becomes traumatized by an event, there is an experience of either fighting, fleeing, or freezing up. This effect can have a lasting experience on the individual.

When we look at the definition of bullying, it refers to a repeated and intentional act that deals with psychological or physical harm dealing with an imbalance of power. Trauma deals with a highly stressful experience in the face of a perceived threat to one's self or to someone close to the individual.

Often when one is bullied continuously, one can develop symptoms of post-traumatic stress disorder. This is especially a response one experiences after a traumatic event like bullying, whose symptoms do not go away immediately. Since bullying is ongoing and sometimes goes undetected, individuals who are bullied develop post-traumatic stress disorder symptoms. We want to create safe environments for all individuals on their jobs and at home by building trusting relationships in their environments.

#30 PSYCHOLOGICAL REPOSITORY FOR BULLYING

When someone gets bullied, one's body succumbs to psychological stress and trauma. Tension, heart palpitations, high blood pressure readings, or shuddering with fear and anxiety overcome the person who is bullied. Very often when trauma occurs at first, it is not even fully recognized by the one who is bullied, and the trauma in the meantime gets registered within our psyches by becoming overwhelming and inescapable. Trauma is a response to a deeply disturbing event that overwhelms an individual's ability to cope with everyday situations. It causes feelings of helplessness in such a way that one's sense of self and ability to fully feel and experience one's emotions is diminished (Onderko 2020). When a person is repeatedly bullied, the person will experience continuous negative reinforcement, systematic abuse of power, ongoing intimidation, and emotional pain. The feelings of powerlessness, helplessness, anger, and fear are correlated with symptoms of PTSD (post-traumatic stress disorder). That is, the person who is bullied may be experiencing and re-experiencing the traumatic event or circumstances surrounding the event and thus has an intense desire to avoid anything associated with the traumatic event (Arzt 2019).

Clara Wajngurt

So it is with this perception that trauma is "stored in the body" (Eckelcamp 2019). It is important to release this trauma through cognitive behavior therapy, relaxation, massage, or similar techniques. When such traumatic events occur, the autonomic nervous system takes over and causes one to appear in a detached manner and frozen state of mind. It is important to find ways to release this frozen state of mind so that the person who is bullied feels empowerment and self-control. After relinquishing the fear, anger, and resentment with the traumatized situation, we hope that the bullying trauma in general is eradicated so that this person will better cope with life's events.

#31 BULLYING AND ANXIETY

When someone gets bullied, it can be a traumatic experience for the target. The pain that a target feels can be so intense that it impacts every moment of one's existence. This means they can feel lonely, isolated, vulnerable, and anxious (Gordon 2017).

Sometimes the target develops anxiety disorders as a result of the constant bullying.

Post-traumatic stress disorder (PTSD) can exhibit in the form of flashbacks, nightmares, being startled easily, or just withdrawing socially from others. When your boss screams at their team and shows uncivil behavior to colleagues, this can possibly elicit symptoms of social withdrawal or nightmares about the boss and other colleagues for both targets and bystanders.

Generalized anxiety disorder (GAD) is exhibited by targets who have worries and fears that distract them from day-to-day activities. If I think that my colleague will exclude me from the team project, I could conceivably develop worries that I am socially excluded from a project that I have expertise.

This disorder can develop to insomnia, restlessness, physical symptoms, and fatigue. The target starts to worry that something bad might happen.

<u>Panic attacks</u> occur when targets experience feelings of terror that strike suddenly without warning. Other symptoms may include sweating, chest pains, or even irregular heartbeats. So an overbearing boss can lead to a target being absent continuously from the job.

<u>Social anxiety disorder</u> occurs when the target is afraid of humiliation or of being seen negatively by others. The target is afraid others are judging him/her. This happens when a personal attack is made continuously about a target on a job. The best way for a target to deal with this situation is to avoid social situations that include the people making personal attacks.

If one is being bullied and has these reactions, we need to seek professional help in order to develop coping strategies that deal with these situations. If your workplace has a bullying prevention policy, this would hopefully minimize the occurrence of such situations.

#32 BULLYING AND STRESS

Imagine the following scenarios:

- Your boss embarrasses you at a team meeting by saying that your work is not effective.
- Your coworker gossips about you and spreads rumors about the visitors you receive.
- Another coworker withholds important information from you for a project you are doing.

Each of these scenarios causes workplace stress for the one being bullied. Suddenly, the target feels anxiety, a lowered resistance to disease, headaches, high blood pressure, and a variety of other physical symptoms. Then all of a sudden the embarrassment caused by your boss causes you to break down, to feel depressed. You know you do great work.

What is going on here?

The rumors spread by your coworker instill an unusual degree of fear and a sense of isolation and insecurity in you and a variety of other psychological/emotional symptoms. Then when you realize that your coworker has withheld information from you for this important project you want to complete, you feel tearful, angry, and indecisive. Soon other colleagues withdraw their support of you and it seems like they have joined in with the bully, which further increases your stress and emotional injury.

Have you felt this on your job?

#33 BULLYING AND PTSD

Any traumatic event including workplace bullying can cause post-traumatic stress disorder (PTSD).

Bullying has a lasting impact on targets, where the targets can experience anxiety, fear, sleeplessness, and depression. This is because the targets feel vulnerable and powerless and cannot defend themselves. Research shows there is a distinct link between bullying and PTSD, which is an anxiety disorder. PTSD results when the target feels threatened directly, or was injured, or was a bystander as a result to such incidents (Gordon 2019). In fact, when the shock of being bullied is so great and occurs at an earlier stage in one's life, then this memory can reappear later on in life as a flashback. PTSD therapy includes three goals: to improve your symptoms, to teach you the tools one needs to deal with the symptoms, and to raise one's self-esteem.

It is important to get the help one needs for working through any experience affected by workplace bullying.

#34 RELATIONSHIPS BETWEEN WORKPLACE BULLYING AND CARDIOVASCULAR DISEASE

I read an article recently about a research study being done in Denmark and Sweden, published in the *European Heart Journal* (2018), that dealt with the relationship between cardiovascular disease and workplace bullying and/or workplace violence.

Eighty thousand adults aged 18–65 who did not originally have a history of cardiovascular disease claimed they were being exposed to violent actions or threats of violence at work. Keep in mind this could include bystander observation as well as workplace bullying experienced by a target.

In general, about 9 percent (approximately 7,200) of the adults said they had been bullied on the job, and about 13 percent (approximately 10,400) said they had been exposed to workplace violence. After a 12-year follow-up, about 4 percent of this group affected by workplace violence (approximately 416) on their job were diagnosed with heart disease or hospitalized for similar events like a heart attack or stroke.

In fact, it was found that for people bullied on their jobs (and affected by workplace violence; 7,200+10,400=17,600), 59 percent (approximately 10,384) were more likely to develop heart disease or suffer from a heart attack or stroke than those people not bullied on their jobs.

This is not saying that workplace bullying and workplace violence cause cardiovascular disease. This says that workplace bullying and workplace violence are big stressors on the job that can possibly lead to cardiovascular disease. Amazing isn't it?

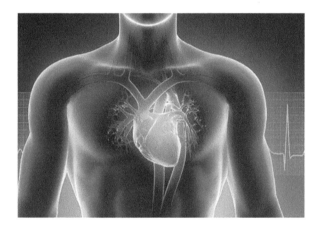

#35 COMBATING STRESS: INDUCED HEART DISEASE

When one is bullied by a boss or coworker, think about it, your heart may be affected. Statistics dealing with victims of on-the-job bullying or violence faced a higher risk of heart disease and stroke (Preidt 2018). It is suggested that if we could actually eliminate workplace bullying, then we could attempt to avoid all cardiovascular diseases due to bullying.

In contrast, the European Society of Cardiology claims that people who were bullied every day during the last 12 months had a 120 percent higher risk of heart disease than those who were not exposed to bullying every day.

Stress-induced heart disease must be stopped by teaching our colleagues stress reduction skills, including muscle relaxation, mindfulness skills training, cognitive behavioral skills training, biofeedback, and yoga. Use of these techniques will calm your reactions in a hostile work environment.

#36 FIGHT FEAR IN THE WORKPLACE

We need to fight fear in the workplace. There is a fear of controlling supervisors, fear of critical staff persons, or fear of demanding clients who can cause mental and physical abuse for the target who is already anxious and intimidated easily.

Change your workplace climate and exercise power and control. Start by advocating for yourself.

Learn about assertiveness training and self-empowerment techniques.

#37 ENCOURAGING MENTAL HEALTH CARE IN OUR COMMUNITIES

It is very important for college athletes to push for more effective mental health care (*Chronicle of Higher Education*, November 8, 2019). Often when a prospective college athlete looks at an athletic scholarship and sets goals for themselves and then falls short of these goals, this can cause anxiety and depression for the athlete after realizing that the original goals may have been unrealistic from the start. In fact, we need to be open to the following statistics: Roughly a quarter of college athletes have experienced symptoms of depression in the past three years. The highest stats were found among female athletes who were track and field—38 percent reported being depressed. A 2016 study by the NCAA (National Collegiate Athletic Association) found that nearly a third of athletes overall felt overwhelmed the month before and also felt mentally exhausted from the demands of their sport. An Active Minds survey found that 91 percent of high achieving athletes with a 3.4 grade point average or higher felt overwhelmed by everything they did in the past 12 months, but only 12 percent sought professional help for feeling sad, anxious, or nervous. We need more support and mentoring from our colleges and our communities to address mental health issues.

CHAPTER 3

Bullying
In The Workplace

#38 HOW TO DEAL WITH A MANAGER WHO BULLIES

The more empowered you are, the more you will not cave into the bully. A bully wants you to react. The bully wants to take away your self-confidence and make you scared. Bullies act the way they do because they seek power and feel insecure. If your manager is the bully and is barking orders, tell your manager the following:

- I can understand what needs to be done. If you talk to me in a more gentle manner, then…
- Do you feel better now?
- Can we move forward?
- I am not sure why you are speaking to me in this manner.
- Enough! I will now…
- Are you interested in continuing this manner of speaking?

What do you think is a good way to approach a manager who bullies you?

#39 CORPORATE BULLYING

If you are a manager of a department and you allow bullying to occur, the following happens:

- The person who is bullied gets stressed, loses confidence, will be absent often;
- The bystanders who watch the bullying will be afraid to speak up, and a toxic culture in the office can be created;
- The one who is bullied will not look forward to working every day and say "Who needs this?" and think "I am leaving";
- The company will need to start looking for other people to replace those who leave as a result of the toxic culture in the office;
- The company will open itself up to litigation and court cases, which will lose money for the company.

Can we not think of stopping this cycle and include bullying prevention conduct in the organizational structure of the corporate environment?

#40 HOW IS YOUR SUPERVISOR BEHAVING?

I recently read an article by Andrew Graham on *Manager Misconduct* (June 2014). An effective manager would do well to avoid the following seven situations:

1. *Lying.* Managers who lie to their team generate rumors that can erode trust and undermine credibility. Stay away from lying.
2. *Bullying.* Managers who belittle their staff create a culture of fear around them. Who can work in such an environment?
3. *Stealing ideas.* Some manages take credit for the ideas given to them by staff members. It is important to recognize positive contributions from your staff.

4. *Playing favorites.* Managers who favor certain people on their staff work with an inner circle that disrespects staff members who exist out of this circle. Not a positive characteristic for accomplishing work deadlines.

5. *Not communicating.* Managers who fail to communicate their goals to their staff confuse the members of their staff about where the team is going in the project.
6. *Managing inconsistently.* When a manager does not follow through on a project, this creates a climate of mistrust and a manager who lacks integrity.
7. *Unsupportive.* Managers who are unsupportive do not act in their team's best interests.

#41 CAN YOU TALK TO YOUR BOSS FREELY?

Joel Garfinkle (2017) in his article describes "How to Have Difficult Conversations When You Don't Like Conflict." When one avoids a difficult conversation, this can impact on your social relationships on the job and off the job. Here are some pointers on how to deal with this situation:

1. Start from a place of curiosity and respect, and stop worrying about being liked. People who avoid conflict with someone they must speak to are often worried about how they appear to others.
2. Respect the boss's points of view and assume they are collegial (you have no reason not to expect this) and they will respect your perspective.
3. Focus on what you're hearing, not on what you're saying. People who shy away from conflict think obsessively about what they will say. Take the pressure off yourself. Mention your ideas and then pause.
4. Be interested and be proactive. Be direct. Address uncomfortable situations head-on! Get right to the point!
5. If you have a concern, talk honestly so that you create a mutually respectful relationship. If you generally have a conflicting culture, sometimes directness may suffice. Be polite. Keep an open and nonthreatening communication style.
6. Don't put it off. Have the conversation as soon as possible if not right away.

Plan the outline of what you want to say and the outcome you expect.

Keep the conversation productive and free from any harassment or bullying language.

#42 HOW MUCH CONFLICT DO YOU HAVE ON YOUR JOB?

Conflict is an unavoidable part of our lives. On the job, conflict results essentially from the following five factors (Farrell 2014):

- Leadership conflict occurs when one boss can be open and transparent, and another boss follows who is more subtle in action.
- Interdependency-based conflict occurs when a colleague needs to rely on someone else's input to get a particular project completed. In this case, we need to clarify the responsibilities of each participant working on the project so people are held accountable and know what is expected of them.
- Work-style differences/conflict occur when some people work well using a team approach, and others work well using an individual approach.
- Cultural differences/conflict refer to a set of values, practices, traditions, or beliefs that certain groups share.

It is important to respect and appreciate that coworkers coming from different backgrounds will experience their job responsibilities differently, whether there are differences in age, race, ethnicity, religion, gender, etc.

Personality clashes occur because we have perceptions about the way someone will act.

For example, if a supervisor denigrates a colleague on a team, the team members may disrespect their supervisor, and the one who was denigrated will feel resentment as a result of the supervisor's denigration.

Unresolved work issues result in job dissatisfaction, depression, and hopelessness. If our colleagues are unable to deal with these unresolved work issues, this can lead to acts of aggression, workplace violence, bullying, and resignation. In the long run, the organization will suffer from absenteeism and increasing turnover rates.

We must help to create a positive and nurturing environment at our workplaces.

#43 WHAT TO DO WHEN YOUR CONVERSATION TURNS NEGATIVE WITH YOUR SUPERVISOR?

You are talking to your boss, who is making recommendations about a project you are doing. Then you are not sure what your boss just said, and you don't know what to do. Should you admit that you didn't follow what the boss said? If you say you don't know, you have a fear that the boss might belittle you or put you down somewhat akin to bullying. What are some options you have?

There is an R-list of categorized tactics to help you deal with this situation (Reardon 2016):

- Reframe the issue from a different perspective, like, "I know you are always good at what you are doing."
- Rephrase the words in a less judgmental way, like someone accuses you of speaking too aggressively, respond by saying, "I am very passionate about what I say."

Clara Wajngurt

- Restate by saying, "There must be another way to say this" or "Did you mean what I heard...?"
- Revisit by using a successful project performed in the past, "You know we work well together."
- Request by asking questions, "Would you clarify what you just said?"
- Reorganize by changing the priority of the conversation. Focus on the process, by saying, "We seem to agree about the situation, but how is this carried out?"

By using these strategies, you can avoid bullying and move ahead with your workplace goals.

#44 WHAT KIND OF PEOPLE DO I WORK BEST WITH?

It is really a fact that one works best with people who behave collegially. However, if they have an attitude and behave disrespectfully to their colleagues, one finds it difficult to team up with such people on a collaborative project. A great reward is to work with people who help you grow professionally. When one works with supportive colleagues and supervisors, one seeks new ways to solve problems, very often in unfamiliar situations.

With a team that works in a cooperative manner, one can take risks and pursue initiatives that are exciting—you work with a purpose and explore different avenues. So if I need to implement new systems or adjust current or existing models at my organization or whatever my assignment is, I hope I can do my job with the support of a compassionate and understanding manager behind me.

When my manager is not compassionate and understanding and has poor social skills, there will be problems for everyone in the department.

#45 HOW DO WE INCREASE WORK PRODUCTIVITY?

How do you accomplish everything you want to do each day? Most of us have issues with work productivity because we have habits that are hard to break and that interfere with work productivity (like gossiping, doing non work-related activities, etc.). Also we are more reactive rather than proactive in the office (we get bullied, we receive negative critique from our coworkers, etc.)

Here are some suggestions:

- Focus on one work-related task at a time and give it your full attention. Prepare a to-do list for the next day and check off what you've done. If you can share your to-do list with someone, that would be great! This way someone you trust also knows what you need to accomplish each day. Cut down your to-do list. If you are starting with twenty-five items on your to-do list, it will be harder to accomplish each task every day. If you want to be productive, focus on the most important tasks on your to-do list. Ask yourself, "How many of these tasks can I reasonably accomplish or make progress on tomorrow?"
- Delegate properly.
- If you assign a task to someone and then supervise each detail of this task while they are doing the task, that's micromanagement. When you delegate, you find someone you trust, who has the skills to do the job, so the job gets done effectively.

- Eliminate distractions. Focus on what needs to be done.
- Break up work periods with exercise or something you enjoy doing, especially some activity that enhances brain function.
- Be optimistic. If you're happier on the job, you'll be more successful.
- Getting enough sleep will have positive effects on job performance.

#46 MAKING MY JOB FUN

Do you want to be sure that your office has the right environment to increase work productivity? If work productivity is maximized, then you and your team can work more effectively together. Consider the following factors that affect work productivity (Johansson 2018):

- *Lighting.* Bright light on a regular basis has been shown to make people happier as well as reduce anxiety and depression.
- *Ambient noise. Ambient* refers to the immediate surroundings of your office. When you hear nearby conversations or are listening to any distracting noises, this can impact on productivity.
- *Music.* Low to moderate volume music has been shown to have a positive effect on employee productivity. However, we need to be sensitive to the type of music and level of sound when it comes to our office neighbors.
- *Air quality.* Poor air quality can decrease productivity. If there are sufficient air filters and therefore cleaner air, this contributes to better indoor air quality.
- *Temperature.* The literature has shown that peak productivity appears to be 70 degrees Fahrenheit or about 21 degrees Celsius.

Be sensitive to our office mates because what is an ideal temperature for one colleague is not an ideal temperature for another colleague.

- *Color.* Research has shown colors have different effects on employee morale and productivity. For example, blue is calming, helping colleagues to dissipate stress, and green dissipates eye fatigue.
- *Existence of plants.* The literature shows that the existence of plants near you can affect work productivity not only by enhancing the scenery around you but by increasing oxygen levels as well.

When we increase work productivity in these ways, it is possible that the existence of workplace bullying is decreased as well.

Clara Wajngurt

#47 HOW CAN LEADERS ON YOUR JOB BE EFFECTIVE IN RAISING YOUR DEPARTMENT'S MORALE AND PRODUCTIVITY?

Every manager in your workplace is pressured to achieve effective results. Today we are competing, moving forward, and always expected to be the best in whatever we do. This pressure situation and focus on getting the job done can cause managers to bully their team for quicker and efficient results. Stay away from bullying by following certain tips. In order for managers to do well, it is important to not only emphasize results but also relationships. You want to inspire your team so they can achieve success and accomplish their goals (Hurt and Dye 2018):

- It's about progress, not perfection. Invest in leadership development programs so you can encourage mentors and leaders in your department.
- Communicate clear, effective, and shared expectations. What is the most important initiative your team can achieve this month? or this quarter? or this year?

- Give your team direct feedback so people know explicitly what to continue and what to change.
- Ask you team, "What is working here that helps you to be productive?" Listen carefully and respond to your team.
- Take responsibility for errors. Apologize, address, and move forward.
- Keep your team focused.

Productive teams cherish trust, connection, and collaboration. Don't allow workplace bullying to thrive. Address this immediately.

#48 UNPRODUCTIVE WORKPLACES NEED TO BE ON THE DECLINE

Best practices in the workplace are always emphasized. If managers and supervisors concentrate on improving best practices, it will be more effective to increase employee productivity and subsequently decrease workplace bullying. So let's look at eliminating conditions that contribute to having an unproductive workplace (McDonald 2019):

- Be sure your colleagues have the space and resources to perform their optimum levels of work. Make sure technology is up to date and employees can handle it. Productive workplaces have sufficient lighting.
- Take a look and determine what is not working effectively in the office—too much gossip and no work.
- Do your colleagues have easy access to communicating with the manager, etc.
- Is the working environment comfortable? i.e., heating/AC sufficient, chairs and tables sturdy, etc.
- Is the manager supportive?
- Are colleagues civil?

Let's defeat these six instances of workplace idleness and increase workplace productivity.

#49 CAN WORKING FROM HOME DECREASE WORKPLACE BULLYING?

Many businesses are open to their employees working at home. Will this affect employees' productivity and team collaboration? According to research it appears that working from home increases employee productivity (Mackay 2000). In fact, the rise in technology use over the years means that employees can complete their assignments on technological devices at home. Team meetings can be arranged via Skype or similar mechanisms, and international connections can be made similarly. We understand that by 2025, millennials will make up 75 percent of the workforce. Because millennials are concerned with a balance in work and family life, many companies are reconsidering their policies about working from home. Here are some reasons that show working from home increases work productivity:

- Reduced commuting time.
- Fewer sick days provides a more flexible work schedule.
- Perhaps less stress at home than working in a cubicle in the office or in an open office where one's colleagues can gossip, bully, or engage in uncivil behavior is better.
- Stress has a negative impact on employee productivity because stress will interfere with one's ability to concentrate on a task and lead to increased job satisfaction.
- Fewer distractions will occur at home—colleagues won't drop by your desk, no worries about office lighting, and no office noise.

- In this way, workplace bullying will decrease and employee retention rates will increase when one's job allows for flexible working patterns.

#50 CAN WE INCORPORATE CIVILITY ON THE JOB?

It is important to come in to work and expect that everyone on your job treats you with kindness and respect. Really we are talking about civility on the job, which deals with a "formal politeness and courtesy expected from our colleagues in their behavior or speech." So what can your supervisor do to ensure that all the people on their teams or in their departments treat each other with civility? (Porath 2018):

- *Articulate values and set expectations.* Managers explicitly set values and expectations from the hiring process and on. Daily acts between employees affect how they relate to one another, and the idea is to create a positive workplace.
- *Managers ought to define civility on the job.* Maintain a workplace statement of civility or code of conduct.
- *Teach your employees skills to understand and respect facility (Cave's Code of Civility).* Greet and acknowledge one another. Say please and thank you. Treat one another equally with respect no matter what the situation is. Acknowledge that our behavior has an impact on others. Welcome feedback from one another—we can be approached by any of our colleagues. We are direct, sensitive to, and honest with one another. Acknowledge the contributions of your colleagues. Respect the time commitments of your colleagues.

If we could incorporate these codes of conduct that represent civility on our jobs, for sure workplace bullying would decrease.

#51 ENCOURAGING CIVILITY IN OUR WORKPLACES

It is important to foster a workplace culture of civility. One way to do this is by including civility in a workplace mission statement and to hold colleagues accountable (Society for Human Resource Management). A leader or set of leaders can galvanize a more positive workplace culture.

Cultivate trust and respectful behavior amongst colleagues. Train and coach employees to increase civility so that job turnover decreases and organizational commitment increases. Establish norms in the workplace like greeting and acknowledging one another or welcoming feedback about work assignments in direct and sensitive ways. In this way, workplace bullying incidents will decrease.

#52 IMPROVING THE EMOTIONAL CULTURE OF YOUR WORKPLACE

Mandy O'Neill from the George Mason University School of Business (McQuaid 2019) gave some suggestions on how to improve the emotional culture of our workplaces:

- Intermittent surveys given to colleagues that reflect how people feel in the workplace about their jobs and themselves as they interact with others.
- Find opportunities that encourage one to get to know your team better. Find out about their personal lives and experiences. What do they bring to the organization outside of the workplace?
- Create microcultures if measuring the emotional culture of your team is too great. Start with a few people. Work with your colleagues' positive emotions and try to spread this around. When there is a culture of positive emotions in your work environment, one is more likely to have improved performance and more innovative ideas.

Negative cultures, which include bullying and other toxic aspects, lead to burnout, absenteeism, poor performance, and high turnover.

#53 SELF-MANAGED TEAMS REDUCE CONFLICT

On the job, many conflicts arise amongst team members. Sometimes the team is given an assignment by a supervisor, and the team doesn't know how to prioritize projects or to react to certain assignments (Maimon 2017). Does the team leader go to the boss, or do you try to resolve the conflict amongst the team members? A self-managed team focuses on the following points to resolve conflict:

- Openly discuss different viewpoints. Encourage openness and transparency.
- When an unexpected solution occurs, do not assign blame to the contributors closest to the problem or issue. Instead, investigate why the issue occurred in the first place than assigning blame in any way. Appreciate the effort and input of all team members.
- Be sure to have all team members participate in the resolution of issues by developing flexible schedules that work for everyone so that everyone contributes to solutions.
  This will allow for positive conversations and feedback from everyone on the team.

Clara Wajngurt

#54 SO YOU WANT TO WORK IN A THRIVING WORKPLACE?

How do you know when you work in a thriving workplace (Craig 2019)? You see colleagues who love and engage in what they do. You're in a workplace where people look forward. You're in a workplace where you can express your feelings. Your colleagues respect one another, and there exists a code of conduct and a bullying prevention policy and community agreements. You work in a place where people are empowered to perform at their best potential. How is such a workplace cultivated? By having inspirational and motivated leaders. Such leadership occurs through your organizational hierarchy.

When your leaders inspire passion, creativity, and innovation, your company will see the bigger picture and embrace the future. If you are a leader of a team, empower your team to use their experiences and skills to accomplish the team project. By incorporating diversity and inclusion, one can reach different talents and perspectives.

In this way, workplace bullying won't thrive in the workplace.

#55 HOW TO STOP WORKPLACE BULLYING ON YOUR JOB?

We all want to stop workplace bullying on our jobs. It is negative behavior and detrimental to the team approach. Let's consider some of these ways to stop bullying (Murphy 2018): Have an idea of how the bully looks. Often workplace bullies are hard to identify. Often they don't yell, threaten, belittle, and sabotage. Sometimes the bully looks great on paper, excellent work. Everyone seems to like the bully, or is it they are afraid of the bully? When the bully looks good on paper, managers overlook their behavior and count it as good performance. We need to educate employers on how to recognize a bully. Establish an accountable definition of workplace civility. Make sure your organization has a civility statement, and confirm that everyone knows that the civility statement exists or a bullying prevention policy exists in the workplace.

Provide job training on workplace bullying. Train your employees to create a more positive work environment. Stay away from toxic environments.

When bullying occurs in your job environment, address it immediately. Have the facts ready when they happen. Hold people accountable when bullying occurs.

Be prepared when talking to the bully. Know how to deal with the bully. You can't make people change, but one can empower others to enforce choices and consequences. Work to eradicate bullying and boost performance on the job.

CHAPTER 4

Bullying
In Education

#56 HOW DOES WORKPLACE BULLYING MANIFEST ITSELF IN HIGHER EDUCATION

Imagine the following scenarios (Wajngurt 2014):

- A unit director submits work to a vice president who makes comments that discredit or devalue the work of the director. The vice president criticizes the director, shows a lack of patience, and fails to demonstrate in a sensitive, professional manner how to proceed.
- A committee is asked to review the state of departmental assessment, but the department chair declines to share significant information with the committee and comes to a committee meeting where he denigrates a committee member for lack of knowledge.
- A faculty member is given an unreasonable teaching schedule. He is emailed his teaching schedule with a note emphasizing that the schedule is not open to discussion.

- The registrar asks the associate registrar to not only compile student registration figures for each academic department but also to write the enrollment management section of the accreditation report. If the assignment is not completed by next week, the associate registrar is told he will suffer disciplinary action.
- The director of grants carefully monitors the professional schedule of the coordinator of grants, imposing restrictive work rules.
- A faculty member in the professorial ranks makes cruel, insulting comments in public about an untenured faculty member's psychological problems.
- In the performance review of a faculty member who is up for promotion, the department chair undermines the faculty member's professional standing, does not identify reasonable means of improvement, and ignores the faculty member's contributions to the department.
- A faculty member believes that she is a target of bias or discrimination in the department. She feels that her professional status is being threatened through isolation and obstruction.

Bullying is an escalating process in which the person who is bullied is in an inferior position. Bullying in the workplace is an act of aggression, and it is associated with high stress levels and a lack of collegiality. The bullying employer demeans, humiliates, and intimidates employees as individuals on a continuous basis.

For this blog, we will use the Einarsen, Hoel, Zapf, and Cooper (2005) definition:

> Bullying at work means harassing, offending, socially excluding someone or negatively affecting someone's work tasks... It has to occur repeatedly and regularly and over a period of time. It is an escalating process in the course of which the person confronted ends up in an inferior position and becomes the target of systematic, negative social acts.

We need to minimize such scenarios.

#57 TERMINOLOGY FOR UNDERSTANDING WORKPLACE BULLYING IN HIGHER EDUCATION

Workplace bullying in higher education is significant to understanding organizational climate and behavior. There are many challenges to addressing incivility in a university environment. Some of these challenges deal with the inter-relationships between faculty, staff, and administration. In order to better understand this, there are some definitions we need to consider.

Workplace bullying (Namie and Namie) is the repeated health-harming mistreatment of an employee by one or more employees through acts of commission or omission that are manifested by verbal abuse or physical or nonverbal behaviors that are viewed as threatening, intimidating, humiliating, sabotaging, and exploiting or some combination of one or more of these categories.

Target (Namie and Namie) identifies the victim of bullying as a target who is the recipient of unwanted bullying.

Very often there is an expressed fear and helplessness to discuss opinions about their situations with others. *Harassment* (Hegranes 2014) is an illegal abuse of civil rights. Workplaces are bound by law to enforce protections to protected classes and to take appropriate actions against violators.

Peer review is a process by which faculty and staff engage in order to advise the university that faculty and staff are eligible for appointment, promotion, or tenure.

Academic freedom (AAUP 1940) protects the rights of professors to conduct research and to present subject matter in their classrooms without fear of retribution.

Tenure is a title that faculty and staff earn through their demonstration of exceptional performance in teaching, research, scholarship, and service to their university.

In order to understand the culture of bullying in higher education and the structure of the university system itself, these terms must be understood.

#58 IS BULLYING A PROBLEM ON YOUR CAMPUS?

The following behaviors may constitute workplace bullying:

- verbal abuse
- nonverbal conduct that is threatening, humiliating, or intimidating
- interference in work or sabotage that prevents work from getting done
- false accusations of mistakes
- hostile glares
- yelling or shouting
- exclusion of individuals
- use of put-downs or insults
- unreasonably heavy work demands

#59 WHEN ABUSE OCCURS AT THE UNIVERSITY

What happens when there is abuse of faculty in a university environment? (*Chronicle of Higher Education* November 2017): Abuse is an accepted behavior when one says, "That's how things are done at this university." This could be in reaction to someone claiming they are being abused where the abuser says, "If you can't take it, then just leave."

Abuse destabilizes targets. It takes a long time to realize that your department chair, who appears generous and supportive, is really isolating you and controlling you. Abuse thrives in the university setting because coworkers enable it. Department chairs stay in power because it maintains the status quo.

Silence and inaction then become behaviors of enabling. It is easier to blame the victim than change the system. This means that the ostracized/isolated/untrusted person tends to blame themselves or others unrelated to the situation for anything that is wrong in the system, when it is really the one in power that causes such incongruities.

Looking at abuse in the university environment can help one to understand why workplace bullying can thrive there.

#60 ENABLERS AND ABUSERS IN FACULTY CULTURE

An article in the *Chronicle of Higher Education* (K. A. Amienne November 2017) called "Enablers and Abusers in Faculty Culture" brought to my mind what exists in the university faculty environment. The fact is that the university is the harbinger for "critiquing bullying, manipulation, coercion and control" wherever it exists in "power structures, gender norms and injustice." But when a person like a department chair or vice president has the power to make or break someone else's career, there is abuse and bullying. As it is a well-known fact that guidance for an untenured assistant professor is needed to achieve tenure, and when the chair refuses to provide such guidance, for whatever reason, the chair becomes both an abuser of the untenured assistant professor and an enabler of workplace politics because the chair does not want to promote this professor. Usually, this occurs if this untenured professor is a scholarly threat to the tenured chairperson. More enabling is done when other colleagues in the department say nothing about this process.

#61 PASS THE HARASSER

Do you know of professors who commit sexual harassment at your university? A sexual harassment situation occurs, the professor decides to resign quickly, gets a new job, and does not refer to any prior harassment at the former institution when applying to another university. This situation is known as pass the harasser. It is now getting more attention by universities and legal advocates.

Sometimes the college on the receiving end is aware of the professor's misconduct and hires the person anyway, especially if the professor is very credentialed in research, teaching, and grants. In other cases, the college on the receiving end does not know about the former harassment committed by this professor at the former college because this is private information and the colleges will not share such information. Sometimes colleges sign confidential settlement agreements with employees who have committed harassment, thereby moving them on without informing the institution on the receiving end with regard to how this employee behaved.

This situation is finally changing and state lawmakers are stepping in to change this law. It will take quite a while to get this into effect (*Chronicle of Higher Education* July 19, 2019).

#62 CIVILITY AND ESCALATION TO WORKPLACE BULLYING IN THE CLASSROOM

Workplace bullying lies on a continuum that starts with incivility, escalates to workplace bullying, and then escalates to workplace mobbing and violence. In this blog, I would like to deal with faculty and student incivility in the classroom.

Those of us who teach in the classroom notice that our students are increasingly coming in late, sleeping in class, using their cellphones nonstop or sometimes exhibiting discourteous exchanges with the professor. It is possible both students and faculty are responsible for these behaviors: students may not feel motivated to learn the material that is being taught, may feel uninvolved and bored, and often faculty have issues in effectively managing their classrooms. If this situation is not resolved immediately, incivility can escalate to workplace bullying between professor and student.

#63 DO PEOPLE WHO ARE BULLIED SUFFER IN SILENCE?

Did you ever feel that when a teacher, a professor, or a supervisor have someone in their class or department who is a bully, it's not the target who is protected but the bully who is protected?

Why does the one who is bullied have to suffer like this? Here are some possible explanations:

- Sometimes bullying occurs away from others so it can be done secretly. Bullies like to wield power so the one who is bullied will not tattle.
- If the one who is bullied tattles, this will make the bully even angrier, so better not to tell anyone.
- The one who is bullied feels shame and may blame themselves for the situation. "Maybe there is a reason why I was bullied," they think.
- Why tell anyone about the bullying incident? No one will do anything anyway.

We need to stop this manner of thinking and focus on solving problems and exposing the bully.

#64 EDUCATION/PREVENTION

Policies on the campus that are made to effectively deal with bullying behaviors are needed. Employees who are bullied report decreased job satisfaction, lower productivity, and potential conflicts with other employees. Particularly, colleges and universities that have experienced recent leadership changes could have large bureaucracies, and a history of tolerant cultures that freely express statements that are not kept in line, and sometimes such environments lead to more bullying incidents.

Freedom of expression and thought are essential to the university climate. However, the rules of conduct need to be enforced in light of a college's mission and goals statements. Leadership at a university must develop clear statements of organizational values, which include a culture of mutual respect.

Perhaps an early-alert program in which administrative departments are coached on bullying behavior is a possibility for prevention. In addition to educating its employees on harassment policies, ongoing workshops for university employees can train employees on supporting bullying prevention behaviors. Sometimes, but not all the time, an objective mediator or someone specialized in conflict resolution and meditation can help. And last of all, we need to advocate legislation dealing with bullying prevention in our colleges and universities, on the federal and state levels, so that leadership on campuses can be further guided when bullying incidents occur on campus.

#65 CREATING A POSITIVE CLIMATE IN THE CLASSROOM IS VERY IMPORTANT

Creating a positive climate in the classroom is very important. So here are some pointers that professors can do to make students feel more connected in the classroom:

- Be positive and encourage students when they speak.
- Treat everyone fairly, and be sure students treat one another fairly as well.
- Keep an open relationship with students. Ask how they are doing. Help the students get to know one another.
- Have an atmosphere where it is okay to ask questions.
- Effectively control the students who don't want to learn and disrupt through motivational activities that demonstrate interpersonal dignity and respect. Treat students with kindness, allowing everyone to share ideas.

In this way, a climate of learning and civility in the classroom can be achieved.

CHAPTER 5

Bullying
In Nursing, Law, And
Graduate School

#66 BULLYING AND NURSES: AN INTRODUCTION

When faced with challenging situations, nurses conduct themselves according to nursing virtues and ethics. However, doing the right thing can be difficult at times, for many reasons. Nurses often face from other nurses the threat of retaliation and unwanted conflicts on their jobs. Specifically, nurses strive to maintain integrity by overcoming their fears to speak up and challenge unethical practices.

However, bullying in the nursing profession is a common occurrence unfortunately, and we need to do something about nurse bullying so that nurses can do their jobs better and help their communities.

#67 BULLYING IN THE NURSING WORKPLACE

Bullying in the health care environment, specifically bullying toward nurses, can result in serious health-related outcomes not only to nurses but to everyone affected, including patients who are under their care.

In Quine's article (2001), we note that nurses reported being bullied more than any other health care worker on staff, physicians, social workers, and other health-related workers at a hospital. Mayhew and Chappell (2001) state that nurses were more vulnerable to bullying than other health care workers because nurses were predominantly female (this may be changing) and they perceived themselves to be powerless amongst physicians, administrators, and other senior nurses who were mostly male.

The consequences of bullying in the nursing workplace can affect interpersonal relationships amongst the workers and the patients, but it will deleteriously affect the organizational climate, quality of patient care, financial loss, and projected image of the workplace in the general health care setting.

What we need to do is for health care workers to better understand this dynamic and to build a framework so that nursing administrators and clinical supervisors can detect early signs of workplace bullying in the hospital environment. This will be done by educating all employees and by increasing one's knowledge about how to recognize bullying in the health care environment. Otherwise, patient care in our environment will be sorely impacted.

#68 WHAT HAPPENS WHEN NURSES ARE BULLIED?

There are many nurses who are being bullied. Some of these bullying behaviors consist of personal attacks, criticism, isolation, intimidation, degradation, belittling, rolling eyes in disgust, hand gestures that steer the conversation, abuse, or erosion of professional competence and reputation. As a result of this, the targeted nurse will lose self-confidence, which could then escalate to stress, physical illness and mental distress or anxiety.

Negative behaviors that make the job of the targeted nurse difficult include having an unmanageable workload, which includes overseeing many patients, receiving punitive actions from a supervisor like posting medical errors on a public blackboard for all to see, or having a supervisor who writes critical evaluations for a nurse. So the impact of bullying on nurses' productivity causes impairment of their physical and psychological conditions.

Power imbalance occurs in the hospital because there are many hierarchical groups—between managers and supervisors as well as between physicians, nurses, social workers, licensed practical nurses, health aides, etc. Berry, Gillespie, Gates, and Schafer (2012) have found that 21.3 percent of newly graduated nurses were exposed to workplace bullying in their first six months on the job, and as a result their work productivity significantly declined.

We need organizational support and commitment to protect nurses' health and welfare from the damaging effects of workplace bullying.

#69 ALLEVIATING NURSE BURNOUT ON THE JOB: CAN WE DO THIS?

About a week ago, I spoke to someone in the nursing field and was told that long-term-care nursing is essentially understaffed. As a result, the nurses in long-term care are forced to work longer hours, and the residents at the facility are often increasing, and long-term care nurses have many activities on their calendars. It is a fact that nurses who work longer hours are more prone to burnout and medical errors (Caulfield 2019). We need to invest in the mental health of nurses. The stress of balancing one's physical health, keeping on your toes, one's mental health, and nurse abuse, including nurse bullying, would affect patient care. Poor communication, lateness on the job, and neglecting one's patient will impact on the overall quality of health care at the facility. It is important for managers to praise and respect their nurses.

If the directors at the facility appreciate the work of their nurses, perhaps nurse disengagement will be decreased. Secondly, work with staffing agencies to hire more nurses. If you are a manager or director, this can alleviate nurse burnout and improve patient outcomes.

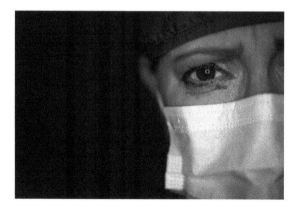

#70 INCIVILITY AND BULLYING IN THE NURSING ENVIRONMENT MUST STOP

In the *American Nurse Today* (Grant 2019), we read that for many decades nurses did not speak openly on the job about incivility and bullying. If they did speak up, our managers and supervisors would say, "It's all part of working in a fast-paced, high-stress environment." Now times have changed and more research is coming out about incivility and bullying. Most nurses view such behaviors as workplace hazards. However, such incidents still arise. The article refers to two specific incidents: one incident is, an experienced nurse who claimed that a physician on her team exhibited unprofessional behavior towards nurses. Another incident is, a new registered nurse contemplated suicide after being bullied repeatedly by her peers. The American Nursing Association's position statement on incivility and bullying reinforces the need to create cultures of respect and provide recommended interventions for nurses and other employees.

We must end incivility and bullying in our health care environment by engaging top leaders in this environment to work together on committees and groups whose mission is to stop this behavior. By implementing effective strategies and reporting incidents when they arise, we will try to alleviate such stressors in our health care environment.

#71 STOP THE GASLIGHTING OF NURSES!

Gaslighting is a technique used by managers and directors to control their staff. In the health care field, such actions from your boss can confuse their staff of nurses and ultimately impact negatively on patient care. Here are some of the actions a gaslighter boss will do (Ciocco 2019):

- *Pretend* not to see you nor acknowledge your work and efforts and at the same time shower you with compliments.
- *Change* project guidelines for their staff at whim, confusing the staff.
- *Invade* your privacy by listening to your conversations, reading your mail, following you around.
- *Tell* you one thing and deny that it was said.
- *Humiliate* you in front of other staff members.
- *Give the impression* they are listening to what you say but doing and thinking something else at the same time.
- *Gossip* about staff members.
- *Lie* about staff member's work or contributions to help a patient and improve the patient's condition.

In essence, if such behaviors are exhibited by your boss on the unit, this can affect one's self-confidence and focus. Patients' health care will likely be impacted by nurses who are affected by such employers who micromanage and make up rules and procedures for different staff members. We need to stop such gaslighting techniques in our working environments. Document everything and surround yourself with colleagues who value your work potential and appreciate you as a person. Such behaviors in the workplace need to be stopped!

#72 ANTIBULLYING WORKSHOP FOR NURSES

I am suggesting an educational program geared for nurses and all health professionals at any hospital in order to ensure their environment is free of workplace bullying. This program should be used as a framework to decrease bullying in the hospital environment and to also meet on a monthly basis to assess how this course is being implemented.

Suggested Workshop To Address Workplace Bullying Prevention In A Hospital Environment

There are basically eight modules in this program:

1. *What Is Bullying.* Definition and basic background of bullying in the nursing / health care workplace.
2. *Negative Behaviors of the Bully.* Varies from personal attacks, attempts to decrease one's confidence, competence or reputation, attacking a target during their on-call work time.

3. *Analyze Power Imbalance from Bully to Target.* How this is described within the hierarchy of the hospital work environment.
4. *How Long Are These Negative Behaviors Exhibited.* For a long time, etc.
5. *What Are the Effects of Such Behaviors.* Poor quality of patient care, turnover rates, etc.
6. *What Are the Psychological Effects on the Target.* Anxiety, depression, etc.
7. *What Are the Physical Effects on the Target.* High blood pressure, aches and pains, etc.
8. *What to Do When Bullying Occurs or Is Witnessed.* Create a bullying prevention policy if the hospital doesn't have one, role-play on a monthly basis communication techniques to reduce bullying, and make this mandatory for all personnel.

What do you think?

#73 WORKPLACE BULLYING IN LAW FIRMS

This is another report on statistics on workplace bullying. According to balancecareers.com statistics may vary from report to report, but some studies show that nearly half of all American workers have been affected by workplace bullying. This means either the person who was bullied was a target or a witness to such behavior.

It is thought that law firms and legal workplaces are also places that exhibit bullying behavior. The fast-paced, adversarial nature of litigation attracts bullying personalities who are very ambitious, combative, powerful, and competitive.

We need more state enforcement of work discrimination laws so that places like litigation firms can talk civilly to people and be respectful.

#74 WHY ARE DOCTORAL STUDENTS MORE PRONE TO BEING BULLIED?

In higher education, we find that students enrolled in doctoral programs are often bullied. First, there occurs social isolation when students are being bullied, because if one comes forward, there could occur possible rejections from professors and staff, especially if the stated perception is not coincident with what the majority feels. There is frustration from bullied students in doctoral programs, because faculty and staff dismiss incidents of bullying as workplace conflicts. Students who complain about uncivil treatment from faculty, staff, or other students are considered as too weak to pursue their doctoral studies or simply troublesome. The bullied students are often separated from others either overtly, like through ostracism, or covertly, like through gossip. As a result, university doctoral students who are bullied often keep a low profile and learn not to interfere with any nondesirable groups.

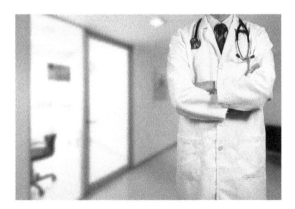

All this behavior is inevitable as a result of the hierarchical nature of the university setting and the social structure of acquiring tenure and moving up the professoriate level. An unbalanced power struggle between two people, like a dean and a professor, pressure to publish or perish, competition for scarce resources, limited accountability, and competitive research agendas, contribute to an uncivil and bullying atmosphere of the university and its doctoral students.

CHAPTER 6

Bullying
Creates A Toxic Environment

#75 DEALING WITH TOXIC ENVIRONMENTS

I recently saw some posters dealing with toxic environments that I thought were very focused (Cole 2019):

- Do you work in a toxic work environment? Does the thought of work stress you out?
- Do you feel depressed or overwhelmed while you are working?
- Do you have a hard time disconnecting yourself from your job when you come home?

If you answered yes to these questions, you may be working in a toxic environment. Sometimes it's hard to tell if you work in a toxic environment or you just hate your job. A toxic workplace will negatively affect your health. It can make you sick. You are more likely to experience depression. You may feel less motivated in general to do anything.

Do you dread going to work?

Does your workplace come with internal politics or cliques?

Is your employer a revolving door where colleagues are coming and leaving? Is there more gossip than open conversation in your workplace?

Is there an absence of trust throughout the organization?

Do you feel uncomfortable disagreeing with your manager or colleagues? Are you pessimistic when someone proposes a new idea?

Think about it, bullying will thrive in a toxic environment. We can stop bullying by eradicating toxic environments.

#76 HOW DO YOU KNOW YOU'RE WORKING IN A TOXIC ENVIRONMENT?

- Your boss says to you, "You are lucky you have a job!"
- When you feel you are left out of the loop, there is poor communication.
- Everyone around you looks miserable. You know something is wrong.
- There is always office drama, people talking and gossiping.
- Do you feel like your meetings are a waste of time? Is there disorganized chaos in your department?
- Does your boss try to control every move you do?
- Do you just feel on the inside something is wrong?
- When you see bullying and harassment going on and people around you keep quitting their jobs and you then feel anxiety and paranoia at work, it's time to think of moving out of your department.

#77 DIFFERENT CLASSIFICATION OF TOXIC INDIVIDUALS

According to Usman (2018), there are many characterizations of individuals who exhibit toxic behavior. The different classifications are very interesting. The question is how to deal with them, as we have been discussing:

1. *The gossip.* "Did you hear about who's getting a promotion?"

    Gossip in the office leads to a decrease in work productivity if too much of this is done. This behavior becomes toxic when the gossip is preoccupied only with such stories. One can say let's talk about this during lunch or after work.

2. *The yes person.* "Yes, that sounds great, if you say so."

    This is a team member who always agrees with everyone at the end of department meetings, never initiating nor bringing new ideas to the conversation nor willing to learn. They put the minimum effort into their jobs, doing only what is expected of them, nothing more. Talk to them and find out why they are so disengaged and lack enthusiasm.

3. *The procrastinator.* "I'll do it tomorrow."

    If you are a manager, be well-defined in your responsibilities and their timelines. Praise people on your team for their efforts and show positive interest when members of your team think through a problem creatively.

4. *The excuse maker.* "That's not my job."

This colleague avoids work, but unlike the procrastinator, who says they will do the job, the excuse maker finds a way to not even do the work—absent from work. Lack of motivation is a reason for this. Hold such employees accountable for their assignments by having them submit periodic reports.

5. *The narcissist.* "Nobody can do what I do."

This colleague is an excellent worker but doesn't understand the value of a strong team. This person loves working independently and doesn't understand that success of the corporation needs cooperation to undertake challenges.

6. *The grump.* "Why do things like this happen all the time?"

This is the colleague who complains about everything all the time. Speak to them and understand what they want.

7. *The sage.* "I know it all."

This is the colleague who has an answer for everything, who won't accept nor listen to another perspective nor any feedback. If employees refuse to listen to critique, they build walls against new ideas and solutions. Incorporate workplace training sessions on civility and collegiality so that the sage can think out of the box.

If you are the supervisor, observation, feedback in a constructive manner, and coaching are the tools for dealing with behavior that is toxic.

Do you work with such individuals? How do you deal with such situations?

#78 HOW DOES A BULLY EXIST IN A TOXIC WORKPLACE?

Ask yourself a few questions with regard to bullying in your workplace (kickbully.com):

Does your workplace confront colleagues who are aggressive or exhibit inappropriate behaviors?

When a bully exists at your workplace, does the manager warn the bully how important it is to follow appropriate conduct and to deal fairly with colleagues? Does your company investigate charges of people who have felt backstabbing and manipulation?

If yes, this is not a toxic workplace.

However, if your organization refuses to acknowledge workplace bullying incidents and rewards colleagues who bully, then a workplace bullying culture exists on your job.

#79 SOMETIMES YOU CAN'T TELL YOUR WORKPLACE IS TOXIC

The article "8 Easy-to-Miss Signs Your Workplace Is Toxic" (2018) implies if we work in a toxic workplace, one can often see subtleties such as lack of appreciation from your manager for the work you have done, minimal accountability for assignments, irritable boss, colleagues feeling bored and uninvolved.

Sometimes, though, the signs of a toxic workplace are not as obvious and are more subtle. Managers and bosses need to recognize these subtle signs so something can be done immediately to tackle these issues.

Here are some examples:

You find out what people really think of decisions reached at their staff meeting after the meeting. During the meeting, almost everyone is silent. After the meeting, colleagues huddle amongst themselves to really tell one another what they thought about the meeting.

Do you have a situation where your arrogant boss talks and talks about what needs to be done, and none of the staff members dare to interrupt him/her?

Your boss only promotes certain people, and promotion is not based on background nor performance.

Do your colleagues talk about whether goals are being met, timelines are being observed—is there an underlying fear of failure and doom if we are not successful in keeping these goals? Or do people discuss collaboration on projects, teamwork, and coaching with one another?

Do you have people around you who don't smile, don't laugh, don't talk to one another inside and outside the office?

Do you find people who don't perform for the given project, and basically don't contribute any work for the assignment, are not confronted?

Do you find nobody cares to ask for your input?

Do you know the vision for your workplace? If you can identify with any of this, you're probably working in a toxic environment that could potentially become rife with workplace bullying.

Let us open up our eyes and change our approach to our jobs.

#80 CHARACTERISTICS OF TOXIC LEADERS: WHY DO THEY THRIVE?

What happens in toxic leadership is that some colleagues agree unconditionally with their boss, and this agreement is not based on quality of work nor merit. Agreeing with the boss is a plus because this shows loyalty to your boss.

Toxic leaders may sometimes be successful, but this success is temporary in moving the organization forward. The improvement is motivated for the toxic leader because their own personal goals are satisfied, and not the common goals of the organization. In many cases whether the actions seem positive or negative, the behavior of your boss exhibiting toxic behavior causes confusion amongst staff who are already experiencing tension and confusion.

The toxic manager is interested only in the view points of the leader (could be the manager himself/herself but not necessarily) and not in the goals of the organization. The primary goal of the toxic leader is self-benefit. They look for recognition from their staff and for their personal financial benefit.

Since toxic leaders are so self-motivated to advance their interests, the boss may exhibit manipulation, intimidation, coercion to advance self-interest. As a result, the staff is robbed of team spirit and positive collective performance.

In order for toxic leadership to thrive, one must have susceptible followers and conducive environments (Rivera-Perez 2012). It is about a destructive individual who wants to manipulate followers as well as a workplace climate in which they expect to get what they want.

#81 TOXIC WORKPLACES ARE HIGH STRESS ENVIRONMENTS

How do you tell if your workplace is toxic (Mirza 2019)? Consider the following tips, assuming some of these pointers are working together in unison:

- People on the job are condescending to coworkers who are lower down, and the higher-up employees treat junior employees with scorn.
- Your boss compares your work to your colleagues' work. This can encourage negative competition, as people view each other's work with disdain.
- Your success is totally dependent on your boss.
- You can't balance your job with your homelife as you are constantly checking your emails from your job 24-7.

- You can't ask your boss for a vacation or time off as your time off revolves around your manager's schedule.
- There is a constant fear of being laid off.

- Your manager controls you, no lunch hour, imposed dress code, and flexibility hours on the job.
- There is a high turnover rate on your job as employees are constantly leaving.
- Someone else in your department takes credit for your work.

High stress environments lead to environments fraught with bullying.

#82 HOW TO DEAL WITH COLLEAGUES WHO EXHIBIT TOXIC BEHAVIORS

Teamwork and collaboration are emphasized in today's workplace. This means top-down decision making is on the decrease and grassroots operations are on the rise (Curnow-Chavez 2018). Grassroots innovation is impacted by coworker networking, which means sharing information directly between coworkers as a form of organizational decision-making. As a result of this emerging dynamic in our workplaces, any dysfunctional colleague can negatively hurt the team approach.

The most common destructive toxic behaviors include the following:

- Backstabbing, criticizing, blaming
- Gossiping and spreading rumors
- Agreement with the boss when the boss is present at meetings, but not afterwards
- Hoarding information, undermining others
- Having personal agendas

Toxic behavior is destructive because it creates unnecessary drama and destruction. Think about it, these behaviors that are toxic remind us of workplace bullying behaviors. It takes one toxic member on a team to destroy the team's spirit. Toxic behavior undermines the values exhibited by the team leader and degrades the team culture. The team leader must acknowledge what is happening on the team and hold the colleague exhibiting toxic behavior accountable. Such behavior brings the team down.

If the colleague who is exhibiting toxic behavior is your peer, try one or more of these strategies:

- Have an honest conversation with your colleague.
- Serve as a role model for your team. Support collaboration, dialogue, and transparency.
- Talk to your boss about it. Have a meeting to discuss challenging behaviors on the team that disrupt the team approach.
- Ensure that the toxic behaviors do not drain you. If they do, this can impact on emotional and physical health.
- Do not allow toxic behaviors in your workplace to evolve to workplace bullying.

#83 RECOGNIZING EMPLOYEES WHO EXHIBIT TOXIC BEHAVIOR: APPROACHING COLLEAGUES AND FINDING SOLUTIONS

We have been talking about employees on your job who exhibit toxic behaviors and who have ingrained thoughts and patterns of thinking and feelings that contribute to destructive behaviors towards others on the job. Employees who exhibit toxic behavior may react negatively in a very defensive and confrontational manner, especially if they perceive they are being criticized. They may play the victim role by attacking others and complaining to others that they themselves have been treated unfairly, harassed, or discriminated in some way. Sometimes employees who exhibit toxic behaviors lack social skills and are hypersensitive. They overact with anger to a situation, expressing hostility easily, not managing stress well, and are quick to find fault in others.

What we need to do when dealing with colleagues who exhibit toxic behaviors is to let your colleague know what behaviors you see from them that you value and appreciate.

It will be important for you to stand firm so that such people are held accountable for what they say. You don't want to manage their frustration. Set boundaries and limits, which means you will need to set your own boundaries and limits for listening to what they have to say. As you build a relationship with someone and increase your interactions with that person, you build more trust with this person and allow them to be close to you. When you draw limits, you are thinking about the extent to which you accept someone's behavior as acceptable, and you then assume it is a respectable way of interacting with them. When you see your colleague as behaving in a way you don't expect, you can assert yourself by saying why are you speaking this way to me.

How do you approach colleagues who exhibit toxic behavior? What if the colleague is your manager?

#84 HOW TO RECOGNIZE TOXIC EMPLOYEES' MANNERISMS

We mentioned in an earlier blog that toxic employees exhibit behaviors that are very harsh and nasty to others.

Here are some ways to recognize toxic behaviors. These are behaviors that are exhibited over a period of time:

1. The targeted person sees each assignment as a hurdle to complete and lacks motivation.
2. The targeted person manages time indiscriminately, missing deadlines, demonstrates inefficient work habits, disorganized—wastes time doing other things online while on the job.
3. The person takes off from work, being absent a great deal, takes a lot of sick days or comes to work sick.

4. The person creates drama in the office, makes things more complicated than they should be, being loud and distracting.

5. Everything is seen as a struggle, complains often, lacks credibility amongst colleagues, disregards protocol, and bullies others.
6. Person may constantly say when a suggestion is made, "It won't work" or "We've already tried this" or "I don't like doing it this way." The person displays a negative attitude.

Do you know colleagues who exhibit toxic behaviors?

#85 HOW TO RECOGNIZE TOXIC COWORKERS: IMPACTS

Have you ever been in a situation where you find your job to be so stressful because one of your colleagues makes life difficult for everyone else? Is it possible that this colleague makes your workplace so difficult it just drains you completely and impacts your work productivity? Perhaps you find that sometimes this person pretends to be your friend and at other times undermines or bullies you in front of others. Away from the job, you can avoid a person who exhibits toxic behavior, but at work, it is just not so easy to do this. What are some signs that you should look for that will tend to make one think your colleague is exhibiting toxic behavior (Titner 2019)?

- They love gossip.
- The secret know-it-all who appears to be a team player when the boss is paying attention but when the boss is not looking insists he/she knows everything and there are no other perspectives.

- They act as if they have paid their dues because they have been at the workplace longer than their other colleagues, so why not let other people do the work.

- They refuse to learn new skills nor to grow nor to adapt.
- They use peer pressure or any perceived influence to manipulate their coworkers and keep people from accomplishing a task, while they insist any success is due to their influence and not due to any collaborative, team approach.
- They assign blame to others when things don't work out as planned.

#86 EMPLOYEES WITH TOXIC BEHAVIOR

How To Recognize Them: Definitions

A lot of us work in competitive environments, and sometimes we even work with colleagues who make us feel confused, anxious, or angry when we deal with such coworkers. You speak to them and you feel disrespected, put down, and sometimes you feel like you're walking on eggshells as you interact with them.

Sound familiar?

You know the less dealings you have with such toxic employees, the better it is for you emotionally and physically. But sometimes you have to deal with such colleagues. According to Bush (2017), a toxic employee is someone who has a "pervasive and ingrained pattern of dysfunctional thoughts and feelings that contribute to behaviors that are destructive not only for themselves but for others."

Often employees who exhibit toxic behaviors are not aware of their negative behaviors and its impact on others.

Sometimes the toxic employee is okay about it. Confronting them in a constructive manner, like "It's not helpful to say all of you are annoying," can be viewed positively by the toxic colleague exhibiting such behaviors. But sometimes such coworkers may react defensively, like "I never said this." Even if they view your statement as critique about themselves, the toxic coworker can resort to bullying the person(s) who expressed this critique, and sometimes the bullying may have to do with the toxic coworkers' position in the company.

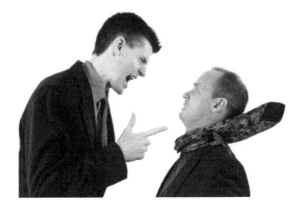

#87 DO YOU ENABLE A TOXIC WORK CULTURE WITHOUT REALIZING IT?

On your job, do you contribute to a toxic workplace? According to Celia Swanson (2019), there are two types of team members at work: passive enablers and active enablers.

Passive enablers are those colleagues who are unaware of what is happening at work. They mean well but are only focused on getting results. They assume the leaders in their organization are trustworthy and have similar values to themselves. On the other hand, active enablers see what is happening but fail to take action. They can best describe and document the problems in their organization.

However, they are hesitant to speak up about what they see because they fear repercussions or assume someone else will speak up or say the situation is not that bad.

It is very important to speak up and be an upstander on the job. If leaders clearly communicate what behaviors and actions are not tolerated, employees will be more empowered and held accountable for their actions. However, if you are afraid to speak up against a toxic work culture, there will be chaos and bullying on the job!

#88 TOXIC LEADERSHIP: WHAT HAPPENS IN THE OFFICE?

George Reed (2002) describes the toxic manager as a manager who bullies, threatens, and yells. A manager with mood swings can set the climate of the office. There is back-stabbing and belittling on a constant basis. It can be the result of whatever you want: poor interpersonal skills, poor office behavior. The problem is if we work for such a person, it can make life intolerable. Such managers put their own needs first. They micromanage and the dysfunctional behavior of such bosses inflicts serious harm on their colleagues. Sometimes it is hard to tell at first whether your manager's behavior is toxic, it could even be a soft-spoken manager too, but the climate that ensues in the office is demoralizing and causes the organization to be ineffective. Colleagues are dissatisfied and are not dedicated to the goals of the organization. There is mistreatment, unfair promotion systems, lack of recognition, and many ethical conflicts.

Can you identify with this toxic environment?

#89 THE TOXIC BOSS FURTHER EXPLAINED

Let's think about your boss. Is your boss destroying your attitude and mood? We have seen research that is described in the book *Dying for a Paycheck* by J. Pfeffer that stressful US workplaces account for 120,000 unnecessary deaths a year (Vozza 2019). A boss sets the tone in your workplace, and when the boss seems overly controlling, untrustworthy, you become stressed and sometimes you don't even know that you're internalizing the stress. If your boss creates a toxic environment, it might be time to look for a new job. But sometimes we can't afford to look for a new job. See if you can make certain changes in your behavior and lifestyle. Focus on the positive aspects of your workplace. Maybe some of the projects you are doing will help you focus on new career goals. Instead of choosing bad behaviors (like eating ice cream or greasy, fatty foods), counterbalance the stress by doing an activity you enjoy or one that relaxes you, like jogging or walking. Take vacations consistently so you relax and get a break.

#90 MORE TOXIC BEHAVIORS EXHIBITED BY MANAGERS

Four specific behaviors exhibited by managers that contribute to a very toxic workplace include the following (Molly Fletcher 2019):

1. *Not celebrating the success of your team members.* Does your boss get excited if your colleague closes in on a big deal or makes an excellent contribution to a project? This may mean more money for your organization. Now why isn't your boss happy about the successes of the team? Could the boss feel threatened that their team member will ask the boss for a raise, or does your boss feel intimidated that maybe they should have closed in on the big deal? The boss ought to celebrate all wins, big and small!

2. *Lack of trust.* When your manager doesn't trust his team to get the job done, then it is possible for the manager's expectations to affect whether a team project moves forward or not. To avoid such mistrust, communicate with your team about what you are feeling and see how the team is approaching the issues, and give constructive feedback.

3. *Afraid of change.* If your manager says, "We have always taken this approach," see if your manager is communicative and will think of using different approaches to solving a problem. Develop a line of communication with your manager so concerns are readily discussed.

4. *All business all the time.* Separate your professional life from your personal life by making time for both. When people feel supported and understood in all aspects of their lives, they will feel more appreciated and enjoy their jobs.

#91 CAN THE TOXIC MANAGER BECOME A COOPERATIVE LEADER?

The cooperative manager is one who allows for free flow of thinking amongst colleagues without a fear of retribution, and employs trust amongst everyone on the team, where everyone has an equal chance of being promoted, generally based on merit or work ethic. Criticism is viewed positively and critique is said sparingly. By demonstrating positive feedback, there is confidence in the team and belief in the efficiency and effectiveness of the workplace climate. There are integrity and moral values and no self-aggrandizement as everyone works together in a collegial and civil way.

According to Rivera-Perez (2012), toxic managers must recognize their shortcomings and need for self-improvement. The team of the toxic boss must have a willingness to openly confront their manager and to offer solutions and assistance without any fear of losing their jobs.

Senior management hierarchically above the manager who exhibits toxic behavior must get involved and provide for this manager, positive mentorship, and monitoring. Proactive counseling and learning how to communicate effectively may be necessary not only for the manager who exhibits toxic behavior but for the team working under such a manager. The idea is to work in a safe and productive environment, and this is the focus.

Have you ever seen a toxic manager become a cooperative manager?

#92 RESOLUTION FOR THE NEW YEAR: GET RID OF TOXIC WORKPLACES

We already know that a toxic workplace deals with a work environment that exhibits higher than usual stress levels. In fact, we already realize that toxic work environments cause mental and physical damage to those who work in this climate.

How do we know when a workplace crosses the line into toxic? Essentially you come home with internal and personal effects of your job that really aggravate you.

It is one thing to have people at your organization annoy you, but when the negativity at work and self-esteem become diminished, your job comes home with you, and you are then feeling aggrieved and lost. This escalates into a problem. You feel disinterested in your job and can't see any positive aspects to your work.

So you connect with coworkers you trust and brainstorm with them on how to make your job more tolerable. People whom you trust have an ability to listen to your comments and feelings. As you talk about how to make this job more worthy for you, you begin to regain that appreciation and respect.

Toxicity in the workplace is out, and we need to fight it when it comes again!

CHAPTER 7

Bullying Solutions
Stop Bullying In The Workplace

#93 HOW TO STOP BULLYING IN THE WORKPLACE

We learn that 35 percent of workers in the United States have been bullied (Jacoby 2016). Since this is a sizable percentage, it appears that this deals with reported cases in 2016.

Let's think of some positive steps to stop bullying in the workplace:

1. *Familiarize yourself with bullying behavior.* What does bullying look like? Repeated verbal humiliation, unwanted critique, isolation, exclusion, and sabotage.
2. *Recognize targets of bullying behavior.* People who are skilled at their jobs, favorites of management, those not particularly aggressive, people who don't interact in group settings are potential targets.
3. *Focus on your job performance and avoid negative comments from others that are unrelated to the job.* Managers should encourage their staff to provide positive constructive critique regarding the task at hand.

4. *Promote a positive workplace climate as a manager.* A manager's leadership will set the tone for how other employees should behave.
5. *Investigate complaints immediately.* Do not ignore complaints or hearsay concerning bullying. The longer a manager waits, the more damage to the target and more liability to the company.
6. *Provide sensitivity training to all employees.* Your employees need to understand what bullying is and how to recognize it. How to investigate a bullying occurrence and maintain confidentiality is very important.
7. *Encourage zero tolerance for workplace bullying.* Very often the bullies are the managers and supervisors and this encourages a culture of bullying.
8. *Identify the incident as bullying, not as incivility, disrespect, or poor management style.* Do not trivialize the workplace bullying incident.

Let's work together to promote these eight points so that workplace bullying is ended in your organization.

#94 HOW TO STOP BULLYING IN THE SCHOOLS

In order to stop bullying amongst adults, we need to get to the root cause of such issues. How about stopping bullying amongst children? People say "Children will be children." But with the rise of more visits to the school counselors' offices and the rise in suicide rates amongst children, something must be done quickly.

Let's consider some ways to reduce bullying in the schools (Crisis Prevention Institute 2011):

1. Make sure your school has a clear definition of *bullying*, "intentionally aggressive behavior that involves an imbalance of power exemplified through physical, verbal, and nonverbal cues over a period of time."
2. Address specific behaviors, such as disrupting the classroom, harassing other students, etc. Do not use labels like, "Your child is a bully."
3. Set rules in a positive framework so everyone knows which behaviors are appropriate. Be consistent in enforcing these rules.

4. Reward positive behavior. This will help reduce bullying behaviors.
5. Maintain open communication with everyone. Let people know you are listening to them.
6. Keep parents involved.
7. Look for warning signs. Are the same children getting into trouble? Do you really understand what happened and why they behave this way?
8. Monitor the spots where bullying can occur, like hallways, cafeteria and often where there is no adult supervision.

If we can tackle bullying in our schools, maybe this will decrease bullying in our workplaces.

#95 NEED FOR A WORKPLACE BULLYING PREVENTION POLICY

Colleges and universities as well as the corporate world and health care organizations must work within their environments to address workplace bullying. While many workplaces have many policies that address specific types of behaviors and abuse like sexual harassment, which is covered under Title IX, a policy that covers threats, intimidation, repeated sabotaging, or negative recurrent behaviors characterized by bullying is not a common policy in the workplace.

We need a workplace bullying prevention policy that will help employees feel less intimidated, who will help people deal with sabotage so that one will feel comfortable reporting behaviors dealing with workplace bullying. These environments will not get rid of the bullies if the bully and bystanders fear retaliation from management.

We need to do something about this.

#96 EIGHT STEPS TOWARDS DEVELOPING A WORKPLACE BULLYING POLICY

When considering a workplace bullying policy, there are certain steps to follow that are suggested for consideration:

1. First one needs to distinguish that the bullying incident is either an isolated incident or a repeated behavior. If the incident is isolated, then this does not necessarily fall under bullying.
2. Is it the management's responsibility to take care of a report on workplace bullying?
3. What is the role of the employees in the department who identify and report incidents of workplace bullying?
4. Confirm that all sources involved with the situation, and any content about the incident, are kept confidential.
5. Who will investigate the complaint or the workplace bullying incident?
6. Describe the specific procedure for resolving the incident.
7. Suggest various ways for resolving the incident and confirm that their resolution will be done quickly and harmlessly.

8. Assess the common risk areas that cause these incidents to occur and present a plan of action for working with such risks so they don't re-occur.

#97 REASONS TO IMPLEMENT WORKPLACE BULLYING TRAINING

It is important for every workplace to provide training for its workers so that sensitivity to possible workplace bullying incidents can be enforced. First, leadership development should integrate a college's job descriptions concerning workplace bullying, including recognition and resolution of workplace bullying behaviors. This means topics such as how to recognize a bully and how to respond effectively to the bully's actions should be included. Also, one should include education about psychologically safe interactions. For example, provide a set of resources of what to do when bullying occurs and how to help raise awareness of workplace bullying for management, union, and all employees.

This encourages everyone in the workplace to be treated with civility. Secondly, provide conflict resolution and emotional training management for all managers that deal with the mental health concerns of the employees, as well as disciplining the expression of their emotions.

Last but not least, managers and staff should be aware of the various leadership styles in your organization, and how these leadership styles can influence the existence of workplace bullying.

#98 OVERCOMING BULLYING

What are some tips to overcome bullying (Ditch the Label 2017):

1. Understand why people bully. Bullying is a learned behavior. Bullying can be a coping mechanism for those going through a stressful situation. This happens when there are deadlines. It is possible that other reasons for bullying can include jealousy and insecurity of the target.
2. Do not get bullied silently. Report bullying. When one is in a stressful situation, it fogs your thinking. One gets distracted, stressed, and unproductive. When a person gets bullied, it is important to seek advice and talk to someone about its occurrence. Deal with the stress of being bullied by talking about it.
3. Don't see yourself as the problem. People experience bullying because of their reaction to the one who bullies. One person can appear as a bully to someone and not to another person. The person with the actual problems is the bully not the target.

4. Even if you want to isolate yourself after being bullied, do not isolate yourself. In general when resolving a problem, look for support. Support will help you deal with the actual bullying and make it easier for you to talk things out.
5. Seek role models. Find positive role models who can inspire you and motivate you.

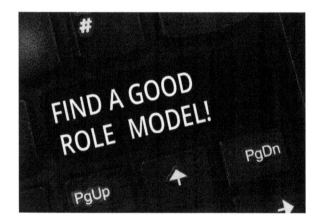

#99 FINDING CLOSURE AFTER WORKPLACE BULLYING

One of the important issues for someone who has been bullied on the job is how to find closure after workplace bullying. In particular, Janice Gilligan White (2019) describes a path of post-traumatic growth after being bullied on the job. Every person who is bullied looks for peace and quiet that brings composure for oneself. If the target does not find that composure, eventually there are health risks. There is a loss of connection to people on the job and a feeling of malaise about the job itself.

The steps to recovery include the following:

- Leaving
- Naming my experience / coming to terms with my experience
- Finding the right therapist/coach
- Getting past the obsession
- Countering the power of bullying by reconnecting
- Finding my voice again

#100 STEPS TO ERADICATING WORKPLACE BULLYING

Generally when workplace bullying occurs, it is an issue whose solution requires the efforts of a majority of all the workers. After all when someone in your department is being bullied, it affects everyone: the target, the people who are bystanders, as well as the manager/supervisor who leads the department.

Even though we generally look to the leader for solutions, workplace bullying is most probably solved by the expression of a collective voice, as Leah Hollis implies in her article on *Preventing Workplace Bullying* (2018). She quite correctly looks at how social change has occurred in our environments.

Although Martin Luther King Jr., Nelson Mandela, Susan B. Anthony, and others represent social change agents and were individually inspirational and dynamic, these leaders could not have effected change by themselves. Each leader worked with a supportive community behind them.

It is the same with workplace bullying. If we are to consider eradicating workplace bullying from our working environments, it is significant to bring voices together so that we not only create antibullying policies but also insist on the execution and accountability of these workplace bullying policies and statements of civility and collegiality.

Can this apply to your workplace environments?

REFERENCES

Chapter 1

Agarawal, P. 2018. Retrieved from https://www.forbes.com/
sites/pragyaagarwaleurope/2018/07/29/workplace-bul-
lying-here-is-why-we-need-to-talk-about-bullying-in-
the-work-place/#6e4c8c4a3259.

Barnhart, B. 2020. Retrieved from https://www.atspoke.
com/blog/support/workplace-empathy/.

BBC News. January 21, 2020. Retrieved by https://www.
bbc.com/news/business-51182651.

Cooper, C. and N. Swanson. 2002. Retrieved by https://www.
researchgate.net/publication/238717808_Workplace_
violence_in_the_health_sector_State_of_the_Art.

Forbes Coaches Council. October 2019. Retrieved from
https://www.forbes.com/sites/forbescoachescoun-
cil/2019/10/17/15-outdated-practices-managers-should-
nt-follow-in-the-modern-workplace/#2b06aa062dbc.

Forte, A. 2011. Retrieved from https://www.researchgate.
net/publication/264842549_How_Does_Organiza-
tional_Climate_Influence_The_Ethical_Behavior_Of_
People_In_An_Organization.

Gluckman, N. 2017. Retrieved from: https://www.chroni-
cle.com/article/you're-not-the-only-one-getting-put-
down-by-your-colleagues-survey-finds/.

Grenny, J. 2019. Retrieved by https://hbr.org/2019/01/4-things-to-do-before-a-tough-conversation 161.

James, L. R., and M. D. McIntyre. 1996. *Perceptions of Organizational Climate*. In K. R. Murphy (Ed.), *Individual Differences and Behavior in Organizations*, edited by K. R. Murphy, pp. 416–450. San Francisco, CA: Jossey-Bass.

Kansas Safe Schools Resource Center. 2012. Retrieved by: https://community.ksde.org/Default.aspx?tabid=3913.

OSHA. 2016. Retrieved by: https://www.osha.gov/Publications/osha3148.pdf.

Perlmutter, D. April 14, 2019. Retrieved by: https://www.chronicle.com/article/admin-101-how-to-become-a-better-listener/.

Pressley, D. 2012. Retrieved from: https://www.sbnonline.com/article/the-importance-of-empathy-in-the-workplace/.

Rodriguez-Hidalgo, A. J., J. Calmaestra, J. Casas, and R. Ortega-Ruiz. 2019. *Ethnic-Cultural Bullying versus Personal Bullying: Specificity and Measurement of Discriminatory Aggression and Victimization Among Adolescents*. Retrieved from https://doi.org/10.3389/fpsvg.2019.00046.

Vaillancourt, A. August 19, 2018. Retrieved by https://www.chronicle.com/article/what-is-your-responsibility-as-a-bystander-to-a-colleague-having-problems/?cid=gen_sign_in.

Vozza, S. 2019. Retrieved from https://www.fastcompany.com/90441594/these-are-the-workplace-trends-that-give-us-hope.

Wolke, D. December 24, 1999. In S. Cassidy, *Beware the "Pure Bully" Who Never Takes Time Off. Times Educational Supplement*, News Section, p. 3

Yamada, D. January 21, 2018. Retrieved by https://new-workplace.wordpress.com/2018/01/21/reissued-for-2018-robin-sterns-the-gaslight-effect/.

Chapter 2

Arzt, N. 2019. Retrieved from https://americanaddictioncen-ters.org/trauma-stressor-related-disorders/effects-be-ing-bullied-harassed.
Eckelcamp, S. 2019. Retrieved from https://www.mind-bodygreen.com/articles/can-trauma-be-stored-in-body.
European Society of Cardiology. November 2018. Retrieved from https://www.escardio.org/The-ESC/Press-Office/Press-releases/bullying-and-violence-at-work-increas-es-the-risk-of-cardiovascular-disease.
Gordon, S. 2017. Retrieved from https://www.verywellmind.com/workplace-bullying-causes-anxiety-issues-460629.
Onderko, K. 2020. Retrieved from https://integratedlisten-ing.com/what-is-trauma/—.
Preidt, R. 2018. Retrieved from https://www.webmd.com/heart-disease/news/20181119/workplace-bullies-can-threaten-the-heart#1.
Xu, T., L. Magnusson-Hanson, T. Lange, L. Starkopf. et al. November 2018. "Workplace Bullying and Workplace Violence as Risk Factors for Cardiovascular Disease: A Multi-cohort study." *European Heart Journal*, 40, 14, 1124–1134.

Chapter 3

Cave's Code of Civility. January 2019. "We greet and acknowledge each other. We say please and thank you. We treat each other equally and with respect, no matter the conditions. We acknowledge the impact of our behavior on others."

Craig, W. 2019. Retrieved from https://www.forbes.com/sites/williamcraig/2019/10/29/10-best-ways-to-build-a-company-culture-that-thrives/#2e47839c7efa.

Farrell, A. 2014. Retrieved from https://yfsmagazine.com/2014/02/06/5-common-workplace-conflicts-every-small-business-will-encounter/.

Garfinkel, J. 2017. Retrieved from https://hbr.org/2017/05/how-to-have-difficult-conversations-when-you-dont-like-conflict.

Graham, A. June 2014. Retrieved from https://www.td.org/magazines/td-magazine/manager-misconduct.

Hurt, K., and D. Dye. 2018. Retrieved from https://www.hci.org/blog/backstage-karin-hurt-david-dye-qa-2018-performance-coaching-development-keynote-speakers.

Johanson, A. 2018. Retrieved from https://www.entrepreneur.com/article/310245.

MacKay, J. 2020. Retrieved from https://blog.rescuetime.com/work-from-home-productivity-data/.

Maimon, A. 2017. Retrieved from https://hbr.org/2017/04/how-self-managed-teams-can-resolve-conflict.

McDonald, J. 2019. Retrieved from https://www.iofficecorp.com/blog/7-poor-workplace-conditions-that-can-negatively-affect-your-workforce.

McQuaid, M. 2019. Retrieved from https://michellemcquaid.medium.com/is-your-workplace-thriving-5fd088b210a.

Murphy, M. 2018. Retrieved from https://www.forbes.com/sites/markmurphy/2018/10/21/five-ways-to-shut-down-workplace-bullying/#29fa0e91e711.

Porath, C. 2018. Retrieved from https://hbr.org/2018/01/make-civility-the-norm-on-your-team.

Reardon, K. 2016. Retrieved from https://hbr.org/2016/05/7-things-to-say-when-a-conversation-turns negative.

Society for Human Resource Management. https://en.wikipedia.org/wiki/Society_for_Human_Resource_Management.

Chapter 4

AAUP. 1940. Retrieved by https://ir.stthomas.edu/caps_ed_orgdev_docdiss/17/.

Amienne, K. A. November 2, 2017. Retrieved by https://www.chronicle.com/article/abusers-and-enablers-in-faculty-culture/.

Brown, S., and K. Mangan. June 27, 2019. Retrieved by https://www.chronicle.com/article/pass-the-harasser-is-higher-eds-worst-kept-secret-how-can-colleges-stop-doing-it/.

Einarsen, S., H. Hoel, D. Zapf, and C. Cooper. 2010. Retrieved by https://www.researchgate.net/publication/291229047_The_Concept_of_Bullying_and_Harassment_at_Work—.

Hegranes, C. A. 2012. Retrieved by https://ir.stthomas.edu/caps_ed_orgdev_docdiss/17/.

Mangan, K. November 21, 2019. Retrieved by https://www.chronicle.com/article/harassment-can-drive-people-out-of-the-academy-here-are-3-ways-colleges-can-fight-back/.

Namie, G. 2003. Retrieved by https://www.rit.edu/~w-aaup/documents_not_rit/ivey_workplace_bulling.pdf.

Wajngurt, C. 2014. Retrieved by https://www.aaup.org/article/prevention-bullying-campus#.X2AR8JNKhQI.

Chapter 5

Berry, P., G. L. Gillespie, D. Gates, and J. Schafer. 2012. Retrieved from https://www.researchgate.net/publication/221837552_Novice_Nurse_Productivity_Following_Workplace_Bullying.

Caulfield, C. 2019. Retrieved from https://www.mcknights.com/marketplace/3-ingredients-to-reduce-nurse-burnout/.

Ciocco, M. June 12, 2019. Retrieved from https://dailynurse.com/the-warning-signs-of-a-gaslighting-boss/.

Grant, E. 2019. Retrieved from https://www.myamericannurse.com/incivility-and-bullying/.

Kane, S. 2019. Retrieved from https://www.thebalancecareers.com/workplace-bullying-bullying-facts-and-figures-2164325.

Mayhew, C., and D. Chappell. 2003. Retrieved from https://www.researchgate.net/publication/267797238_Workplace_Violence_in_the_Health_Sector_A_Case_Study_in_Australia.

Quine, L. 2001. Retrieved from https://journals.sagepub.com/doi/10.1177/135910530100600106.

Chapter 6

Bush, D. 2017. Retrieved from https://www.linkedin.com/pulse/toxic-employees-6-steps-stop-them-tracks-douglas-w-bush-m-a-/.

Cole, J. 2019. Retrieved from https://careerbuzz.prosky.co/articles/how-to-deal-with-a-toxic-work-environment.

Curnow-Chavez, A. 2018. Retrieved from https://hbr.org/2018/04/4-ways-to-deal-with-a-toxic-coworker.

Fletcher, M. 2019. Retrieved from https://mollyfletcher.com/4-characteristics-toxic-workplace/.

Kickbully.com. 2009. "Identifying a Toxic Workplace." Retrieved from https://kickbully.com/toxic.html.

Mirza, B. 2019. Retrieved from https://www.shrm.org/resourcesandtools/hr-topics/employee-relations/pages/toxic-workplace-culture-report.aspx.

Mautz, S. 2018. Eight-Easy-to-Miss-Signs Your Workplace Is Toxic. Retrieved from: https://www.inc.com/scott-mautz/8-easy-to-miss-signs-your-workplace-is-toxic.html.

Pfeffer, J. 2018. *Dying for a Paycheck.* California: Harper Business.

Reed, G. 2002. Retrieved from https://hbr.org/2019/08/are-you-enabling-a-toxic-culture-without-realizing-it.

Rivera-Perez, H. 2012. Retrieved from https://www.academia.edu/28919210/Toxic_Leadership_The_Organizational_Culture_and_Toxic_Leadership.

Swanson, C. 2019. Retrieved from https://hbr.org/2019/08/are-you-enabling-a-toxic-culture-without-realizing-it.

Titner, E. 2019. Retrieved from https://www.thejobnetwork.com/8-signs-your-coworker-is-toxic/.

Usman, M. 2018. Retrieved from https://www.researchgate.net/publication/327743583_How_to_Manage_Toxic_Employees_in_an_Organization—.

Vozza, S. 2019. Retrieved from:https://www.fastcompany.com/90390672/your-bad-boss-is-having-real-consequences-on-your-health.

Chapter 7

Crisis Prevention Institute. 2011. Retrieved from https://www.crisisprevention.com/Blog/10-Ways-to-Help-Reduce-Bullying-in-Schools.

Ditch the Label. 2017. Retrieved from https://www.ditchthe-label.org/wp-content/uploads/2020/05/The-Annual-Bullying-Survey-2017-2.pdf.

Gilligan-White, J. 2019. Retrieved from https://www.freespiritedme.com/closure-after-workplace-bullying/.

Hollis, L. 2018. *Preventing Workplace Bullying.* Retrieved from https://academeblog.org/2018/10/02/preventing-work-place-bullying/.

Jacoby, M. 2016. Retrieved from: https://www.huffpost.com/entry/8-steps-to-take-to-stop-b_b_12630016.

ABOUT THE AUTHOR

Clara Wajngurt is a professor of mathematics, executive coach, author, and speaker who is an expert in the self-development of others and in empowering those around her. She has written several peer-reviewed articles on workplace bullying and believes that when people work together as a team, success will always ensue. Her motto is, "strong leadership, collaboration, and effective communication will lead to dignity and respect for one another."

CPSIA information can be obtained
at www.ICGtesting.com
Printed in the USA
JSHW032041250722
28551JS00005B/90